**Alonso Ortega**

**Malingering**

.

Alonso Ortega

# Malingering

## A Bayesian approach for effort assessment

Südwestdeutscher Verlag für Hochschulschriften

## Impressum / Imprint

Bibliografische Information der Deutschen Nationalbibliothek: Die Deutsche Nationalbibliothek verzeichnet diese Publikation in der Deutschen Nationalbibliografie; detaillierte bibliografische Daten sind im Internet über http://dnb.d-nb.de abrufbar.

Bibliographic information published by the Deutsche Nationalbibliothek: The Deutsche Nationalbibliothek lists this publication in the Deutsche Nationalbibliografie; detailed bibliographic data are available in the Internet at http://dnb.d-nb.de.

Coverbild / Cover image: www.ingimage.com

Verlag / Publisher:
Südwestdeutscher Verlag für Hochschulschriften
ist ein Imprint der / is a trademark of
OmniScriptum GmbH & Co. KG
Heinrich-Böcking-Str. 6-8, 66121 Saarbrücken, Deutschland / Germany
Email: info@svh-verlag.de

Herstellung: siehe letzte Seite /
Printed at: see last page
**ISBN: 978-3-8381-3920-3**

Zugl. / Approved by: Muster: Bielefeld, Universität Bielefeld, Diss., 2013

# MALINGERING: A BAYESIAN APPROACH FOR

# EFFORT ASSESSMENT

# TABLE OF CONTENTS

# TABLE OF CONTENTS

# 1 PREFACE

This book summarizes four years of research at the University of Bielefeld under the supervision of Prof. Dr. Hans Markowitsch and Prof. Dr. Martina Piefke. This endeavor would not have been possible without the important contribution of Prof. Dr. Eric-Jan Wagenmakers (University of Amsterdam) and Prof. Dr. Michael D. Lee (University of California – Irvine). Equally important was the collaboration of our research interns Stephan Labrenz, Christian Poth, Ronja Boege, Jasmin Faber, Shaline Kockmann, Amelie Nikstat, and Verena Wittenberg.

The present work introduces a novel *Bayesian latent group model*, which was developed to determine the presence of poor effort in the context of malingering assessment. In the past two decades, different methods have been developed and used to detect the presence of poor effort during neuropsychological testing. Among these methods, standard neuropsychological tests have been used as embedded effort indicators. Later, malingering researchers developed stand-alone effort measures.

Currently, effort assessment has reached great attention, and prominent professional neurpsychological societies (e.g., American Academy of Clinical Neuropsychology, AACN; National Academy of Neuropsychology; NAN) recommend their use in every neuropsychological assessment. For this reason, effort measures should be periodically revised and improved. Within this context, in recent years some statistical methods have been introduced to determine the presence of poor effort.

In three empirical studies, the classification accuracy of the Bayesian latent group model was evaluated. In Study 1 the Bayesian model was implemented to distinguish between participants that were either feigning some degree of cognitive impairment or performing at their best during effort testing. In Study 2, the aim was to validate the diagnostic accuracy of the Bayesian model against two well established and widespread effort measures: The Test of Memory Malingering (TOMM), and b) the Word Memory Test (WMT). In Study 3, the accuracy of the Bayesian model was evaluated including two samples of patients with moderate to severe cognitive impairment.

Overall findings are strightforwarding and suggest the utility of a Bayesian latent group to complement the existing effort measures in applied field (e.g., both, clinical and medico-legal settings). Even considering these findings as positive, we remain cautious and prepared to conduct futher investigation in this area. The high complexity of both malingering and effort phenomena should be considered. Although findings promote certain optimism, it is necessary to provide cumulative evidence that may recommend the implementation of the present Bayesian model in standard neuropsychological assessment.

Alonso Ortega G.

Valparaíso, September, 2014

# 2 INTRODUCTION

In clinical assessment, it is usually assumed that patients provide genuine and reliable information about their symptoms. This idea is based on the belief that patients are expecting to relieve from their complaints and feel better; however, this is not always the case. Depending on the evaluation context, it may occur that patients try to minimize or exaggerate their real complaints motivated by diverse reasons (Boone, 2007). One particular case has been described as malingering and has been defined as "the intentional production of false or greatly exaggerated symptoms for the purpose of attaining some identifiable external reward" (American Psychiatric Association, 1994).

In 1999, Slick, Sherman and Iverson proposed some standards to determine the presence of "Malingered Neurocognitive Dysfunction" (MND; i.e., malingering). Slick et al. (1999) criteria include results of especially developed effort measures as an important component to determine the presence of malingering. Effort has been conceptualized as the "intentional underperformance during neuropsychological assessment" (Iverson, 2003, 2006). To improve the assessment of effort, researchers in neuropsychology have developed different techniques and methods for its evaluation.

Currently, guidelines and consensus proposed by established neuropsychological associations (e.g., American Academy of Clinical Neuropsychology, AACN; National Academy of Neuropsychology; NAN) endorse the use of effort measures to validate examinees' performance (Bush et al., 2005; Heilbronner et al., 2007, Heilbronner, Sweet, Morgan, Larrabee, & Millis, 2009).

In this context, a Bayesian approach was used to assess effort in the context of neuropsychological evaluation. Within psychology, Bayesian models have been used in data analysis for functional neuroimaging research on memory and other cognitive functions (Ahn, Krawitz, Kim, Busenmeyer, & Brown, 2011; Piefke, Onur, & Fink, 2010; Piefke, Weiss, Zilles, Markowitsch, & Fink, 2003; Schulte-Rüther, Markowitsch, Fink, &

Piefke, 2007), analysis of recognition memory (Dennis, Lee, & Kinnell, 2008), human inductive learning and generalization (Tenenbaum, Griffiths, & Kemp, 2006) and causal learning and inference (Steyvers, Tenenbaum, Wagenmakers, & Blum, 2003).

In three experimental studies, a Bayesian Latent Group model was implemented to identify examinees displaying poor effort during testing. This Bayesian model also quantifies the confidence with which each participant is classified and estimates the base rates of malingering from the observed data. Diagnostic accuracy of the proposed Bayesian model is estimated in both healthy participants and cognitively impaired patients. Given the complexity of malingering and effort determination, the present research also aims at contributing to the improvement of the existing effort assessment techniques.

The following sections provide a *Theoretical Background* including pertinent definitions, a brief description of detection strategies used in malingering detection and an overview of Bayesian methods. Subsequently, a summary of each *Empirical Study* is provided. Finally, the *Concluding Discussion* further integrates the main findings of this research, stating their clinical relevance, limitations and further directions that may orient future studies.

# 3 THEORETICAL BACKGROUND

3.1 Malingering: History, Definitions and Proposed Standards for its Determination

*3.1.1 A Brief History*

It might seem reasonable to assume that illness simulation is as old as humankind (Wessely, 2003). Since people live in societies with duties and obligations, individuals might get involved in different kinds of deceptive behaviors as a pretext to avoid some of those obligations. Hall and Poirier (2001) suggest that during childhood people acquire a basic awareness of deceptive behavior, which is reinforced by social and cultural values. Indeed, Vrij (2001) asserts that deceit is an essential part of our everyday social interactions. However, deception is a broad category that involves different kinds of behaviors such as fraud, prejury, forgery, lying and malingering, among others.

The term malingering originates in the military, and has been used in this context to describe the simulation of injury or illness as an attempt to avoid war duties (Palmer, 2003). As Palmer stated, "Feigning illness is behavior indulged in by all ranks in all armed forces of all nations" (2006, p.22). In Homer's epic poem, Ulysses (Lat. Ulyssês, Ulixês) feigned insanity in order to escape from the Trojan War although Palamedes detected his deception attempt (Glueck, 1916). In ancient Greek, illness simulation as a means of evading military duties was punishable with death (Mendelson & Mendelson, 2004). Notwithstanding, malingering has not been restricted exclusively to the military. For instance, Queen Elizabeth I (1485-1603) feigned illness on several occasions to avoid dangerous and life-threatening situations.

In the 17th century, malingering became a great concern of writers on medical jurisprudence (Nicholson & Martelli, 2007). As a matter of fact, Zacchiae Pauli wrote *"Qvaestiones Medico-Legales"* (1621), which was probably the most influential work on illness simulation (Mendelson & Mendelson, 2004). However, it was only until the 19th century that malingering becomes an issue of major concern in North America and the industrialized societies of Western Europe, particularly Germany and England. With the advent of the modern welfare state, progressive legislation about social insurance issues concerning sickness, accident, old age, and disability, were approved to reivindicate worker class rights (Wessely, 2003). The approval of these workmen's compensation acts caused mistrust and represented a threat among the most conservative spheres of the medical profession. Under this new legislation, many physicians viewed any increase of claims as a proof of the disadvantages of the new system. Indeed, between 1880 and 1900 German neurologists tended to classify about one-third of cases of so-called "functional nervous disease" as due to malingering (Wessely, 2003). By the beginning of the First World War illness simulation reached even higher levels of concern among regimental medical officers and physicians.

Both the emergence of the welfare state, and the impact of the First World War, placed the physician in a key role and malingering becomes medicalized. In this context, the physician becomes a sort of detective and, in its role, used intuition and a repertoire of clinical tricks and traps to detect any attempt of deception. As gatekeepers, physicians had to devise and include new methods to detect malingering. Among them, it can be mentioned the use of chemical analyses, and the extended use of X-ray to determine the presence or absence of diseases (Cooter, 1998). In 1915, many physicians faced an increasing amount of soldiers whose signs and symptoms could not be explained by conventional injury. The introduction of terms such as *shell shock*, *traumatic neurosis*, or *war neurosis* extended the horizons of the medical profession into the psychological domain, and brought about the psychologization of malingering (Cooter, 1998).

Now, it was the effect of war on soldier's minds that constitutes the major challenge to the physicians. As expected, it was not easy to distinguish between malingering and real psychological disturbances due to war stress. After the war, and up to date, the medical and psychological interest on malingering remained as a matter of concern in clinical and medico-legal settings. Over the past 20 years, different malingering conceptualizations, detection strategies and diagnostic standards have been proposed and revised. Because of its impact on clinical assessment, medico-legal issues and social policies, malingering becomes also a relevant and prolific field of research.


*3.1.2 Definition*


The word *malingerer* apparently derives from the French "malingre" (i.e., sickly or feeble), and it was first introduced in 1785 in the *Grove's Dictionary of the Vulgar Tongue* (Mendelson & Mendelson, 2004). Malingering has been defined in several different ways (Iverson 2003). The introduction of the term malingering into medical terms during the 20th century contributed to the establishment of disorder-oriented definitions, and malingering was viewed from a pathological perspective. That is, "if you malingered, you must be sick", and it was considered as an abnormal behavior that needed to be treated (Iverson, 2003).

The Diagnostic and Statistical Manual of Mental Disorders, in its previous edition (DSM-IV-TR), defines malingering as "the intentional production of false or grossly exaggerated physical or psychological symptoms, motivated by external incentives such as avoiding military duty, avoiding work, obtaining financial compensation, evading criminal prosecution, or obtaining drugs (p.739). Even though the DSM-IV-TR does not explicitly consider "malingering" as a mental disorder, it is included in the section "Additional Conditions that May Be a Focus of Clinical Attention" (V65.2 Malingering). Rogers (1990) criticized this disorder-oriented definition, and discussed the transition for a more adaptive conceptualization. During the past ten years, Iverson paraphrased the DSM-IV (1994) definition of malingering as "the intentional production of false or greatly exaggerated symptoms for the purpose of attaining some identifiable external reward" (2003, p.138; 2006, p.78; 2008, p.126; 2010, p.94). This definition clearly summarizes the two main ideas behind malingering, which are: a) the intentional (i.e., conscious) production or exaggeration of symptoms, b) motivated by the presence of an identifiable external incentive.

However, a holistic perspective of malingering requires both, to consider its adaptive nature, and to be understood as a continuum rather than taxonomy. Firstly, malingering may be interpreted as an adaptive behavior. Rogers (1990) proposed an adaptational model in which malingering is considered "an adaptive response to adverse circumstances which may be best understood in the context of decision theory" (p. 327). That is, under determined circumstances, and underlying motivations a person might display a broad variety of responses, being malingering one more possible behavior. According to Rogers (2008), "malingerers attempt to engage in a cost-benefit analysis by choosing to feign psychological impairment" (p.9). The volitional nature of malingering allows for a conceptualization that recognises the capacity of free will, and the decision for seeking benefits associated with the sick role.

Secondly, malingering is not a categorical phenomenon (i.e., all or nothing), and may be better represented as a continuum that varies in its manifestation. For instance, Resnick (1984, 1997) has distinguished and proposed three different types of malingering. This conceptualization includes a) false imputation, b) partial malingering, and c) full malingering. False imputation occurs when someone attributes symptoms to an etiologically unrelated cause (e.g. when an employee attributes bad performance in work to concentration problems instead of alcohol abuse). Partial malingering occurs when patients describe past symptoms that they no longer have or exaggerate actual symptoms. Full malingering is the type of malingering that is usually determined by most clinicians, and refers to the complete fabrication and gross exaggeration of mental or physical symptoms motivated for external purposes. Even though, all of them can be considered forms of malingering, there is general agreement that exaggeration of existing symptoms is more frequent than pure (i.e., full) malingering (Miller, 1996) in either clinical or forensic settings (Iverson, 2007). The nature of malingering as a phenomenon that occurs in a graded continuum has been emphasized by several authors (e.g., Iverson, 2010; Millis, 1994; Rogers, 1988, 1990; Zielinsky, 1994; Walters et al., 2008).

Finally, the concept of volition (i.e., conscious, self-directed behavior), and the nature of incentives (i.e., external vs. internal) are crucial elements that contribute for an adequate differential diagnosis between malingering and some clinical disorders involving symptom exaggeration or fabrication. The current edition of Campbell's Psychiatry Dictionary (2009) states, "[in malingering] external incentives provide the motive for symptom production, in contrast to factitious disorders, and other somatoform disorders, where incentives are internal and related to emotional or intrapsychic conflict" (pp.574-575). In 2007 Boone suggested, "The most problematic differential diagnosis would appear to be between somatoform disorder and malingering" (p.30). Even though Resnick (1984) stated, "No other syndrome is as easy to define,.but difficult to diagnose" (p.23), it can be argued that "no other behavior is either hard to define and to determine than malingering".

### 3.1.3 Malingering-Related Terms

During the past 25 years - in the scientific literature - a plethora of terms have been used interchangeably to refer malingering. For instance, terms such as *"simulation"* (Merckelbach, Smeets, & Jelicic, 2009; Wiggins & Brandt, 1988), *"feigning"* (Bolan, Foster, Schmand, & Bolan, 2002; Blaskewitz, Merten, & Brockhaus, 2009), *"faking"* (Baker, Hanley, Jackson, Kimmance, & Slade, 1993; Hanley, Baker, & Ledson, 1999), *"deception"* (Nagle, Everhart, Durham, McCammon, & Walker, 2006), *"symptom exaggeration"* (Sullivan, May, & Galbally, 2007; Rohling, Allen, & Green, 2002), *"negative response bias"* (Ardolf, Denney, Houston, 2007; Merten, Friedel, Mehren, & Stevens, 2007), *"noncredible performance"* (Boone, Lu, & Wen, 2005), *"suboptimal performance"* (Brockhaus & Merten, 2004), *"suboptimal effort"* (Rohling et al., 2002) and *"poor effort"* (Lange, Iverson, Sullivan, & Anderson, 2006; Lange, Pancholi, Bhagwat, Anderson-Barnes, & French, 2012).

Nicholson & Martelli (2007) asserted that this conceptual heterogeneity produced some degree of confusion among practitioners and researchers. Consequently, misunderstandings about the proper use of term malingering may bring about some undesirable effects on diagnosis and research findings (Nicholson & Martelli, 2007). Iverson (2006), hypothesized that this confusion may occur because malingering, poor effort and exaggeration often overlap, conceptually and in an assessment context (see *Figure 1*).

Iverson (2006, 2008) suggested that the term exaggeration may be less ambiguous if it is used to describe symptom reporting during interview, symptom endorsement on psychological tests or behavioral observations. Poor effort, on the other hand, may be better used to describe individuals' behavior during testing. This simply means the person underperformed during testing. Therefore, Iverson (2006, 2008) suggested the use of the term "poor effort" to describe underperformance during testing, and "exaggeration" to refer over-reported symptoms in a clinical interview.context. This disambiguation may result crucial to estimate the presence of malingering, following the current guidelines and proposed standards.

*3.1.4 Proposed Standards to Determine Malingering*

In 1999 Slick, Sherman, and Iverson proposed some diagnostic standard criteria to determine the presence of "Malingered Neurocognitive Dysfunction" (MND). Slick et al. criteria include:   a) Presence of substantial external incentive, b) evidence from neuropsychological functioning, c) evidence from patient self report, and d) behavior meeting criteria a) and c) that are not fully accountable by knowing psychiatric, neurological or developmental factors. Based on these criteria three different diagnoses can be proposed: Definite MND, Probable MND and Possible MND.

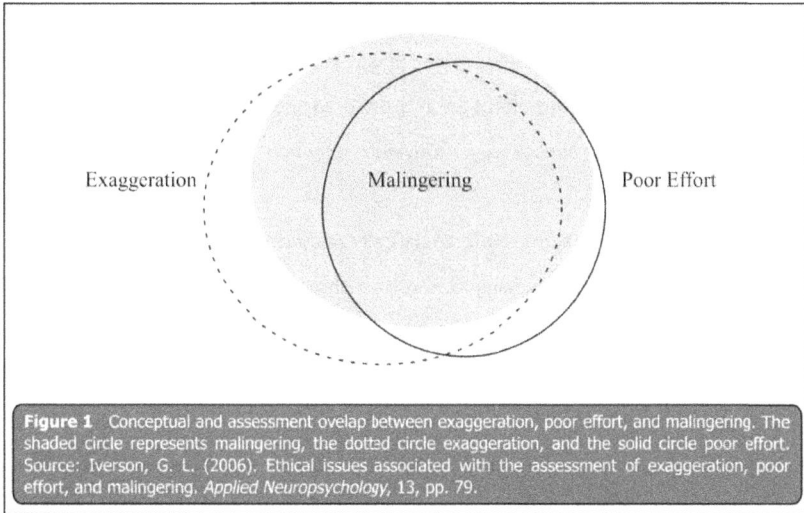

**Figure 1** Conceptual and assessment ovelap between exaggeration, poor effort, and malingering. The shaded circle represents malingering, the dotted circle exaggeration, and the solid circle poor effort. Source: Iverson, G. L. (2006). Ethical issues associated with the assessment of exaggeration, poor effort, and malingering. *Applied Neuropsychology, 13*, pp. 79.

It must be pointed out that criterion a) must be present to determine any malingering diagnosis but should be accompanied by any b), c) or d) criteria (Slick et al., 1999).

During the last decade, Slick et al. criteria became into a standard in most malingering related research, and have been widely used in research, clinical assessment and forensic practice. However, Boone (2007) recently revised Slick et al. criteria, and after performing a thorough analysis, some suggestions have arisen. One important recommendation is to use the term "determination of Noncredible Neurocognitive Function" (NNF) instead of "diagnosis of Malingered Neurocognitive Dysfunction" (MND). This suggestion relies on the difficulty to rule out somatoform disorders from malingering. Frequently, clinicians make the mistake of assuming that the presence of malingering contraindicates the presence of genuine psychopathology. Nevertheless, distinguishing between somatoform disorder, factitious disorder, and malingering is difficult because they can occur together (Gerson & Fox, 2006). Another argument that favors the modification of the current terminology is the inexistence of reliable methods to determine the intentional-volitional nature of the malingered behavior. As long as the intentionality cannot be clearly demonstrated by objective measures we must be prudent when determining malingering. However, this topic can be controversial, especially if we consider that it is apparently impossible to infer the level of consciously mediated intention and there are no reliable or valid methods for objectively determining consciously motivated intention (Halligan, Bass, & Oakley, 2003).

Another important suggestion, specifically related to criterion b), is that definite NNF should be determined by failure on at least three validated stand-alone measures (i.e., effort measures) with minimal shared variance and high specificity, plus behavioral evidence of noncredible symptoms. The last recommendation is not to warn patients about the presence of effort measures within the neuropsychological batteries in order to encourage them to perform with their best efforts. Nevertheless, some ethical dilemmas might appear. In particular, those related to the informed consent that must be given to the examinee prior to any evaluation. Anyhow, this issue will not be discussed here.

Larrabee, Greiffenstein, Grewe, & Bianchini (2007) have also revised and refined Slick et al. criteria. As Boone (2007) recommended determining definite NNF, they suggested allowing multiple psychometric findings to define probable malingered neurocognitive dysfunction (MND). Another important recommendation is to give criterion c) equal weight than criterion b) when diagnosing MND. The underlying rationale is that discrepancies between patient's self-reported symptoms and documented history or behavioral observations are equally important as test-centered inconsistencies. Accordingly, they should be equally considered when determining probable malingered dysfunction. The next section describes different detection strategies used to determine the presence of malingered-related poor effort.

3.2 Malingering Detection Strategies

As previously mentioned both First World War and the increasing legislation about social insurance issues in North America and Europe placed physicians, and then psychologists, as gatekeepers for detecting simulated illness. Under this new role, physicians used a variety of strategies and techniques to determine when someone was suspected of feigning physical or mental complaints. Well into the twentieth century, interest on malingering assessment kept more adepts and new detection strategies were developed.

Zago, Sartori, & Scarlato (2004) described a very innovative procedure used by an Italian clinician (1927) to determine the presence of malingering in a medico-legal context. Several clinicians and renowned academics evaluated an unknown 45-year-old man who manifested severe memory complaints. Until then, not a single clue that might have been used to suggest the presence of malingering was available. Despite this, the neuropsychiatrist Alfredo Coppola (1888-1957) was able to propose and determine the presence of "malingered retrograde amnesia" after implementing language, attention, visual recognition, and different memory tasks (e.g., anterograde, retrograde autobiographical, procedural, semantic and visual imagery).

Later, in early sixties, Spreen and Benton published one of the first studies on malingering about a case of simulated cognitive impairment (Spreen & Benton, 1963). In their study it was shown that normal subjects, who were instructed to simulate cognitive deficits, performed significantly worse than patients with actual cognitive impairment in a visual memory test. Following this tendency, since mid-eighties and until today, different detection strategies have been developed and continuously revised. However, there are two main approaches that can be clearly differentiated. One is the use of detection strategies embedded in standard neuropsychological measures (i.e., embedded validity indicators), and the other is the use of specially developed measures to detect malingering-related poor effort (i.e., stand-alone measures). The following subsections briefly describe both approaches.

*3.2.1 Embedded Validity Indicators*

Indicators of symptom validity can be obtained from the application of standard neuropsychological tests in different cognitive domains. These indicators are usually called embedded validity indicators (EVI). During the nineties a considerable amount of research was conducted to explore the utility of EVI to detect malingering (Berry, & Schipper, 2008). Some of their potential advantages are: a) serving multiple purposes simultaneously (i.e., assessment of both genuine and feigned deficits), b) allowing retrospective evaluations of response validity in previous examinations (e.g., Larrabee, Millis, & Meyers, 2008), and c) providing some protection against coaching. Since EVI do not require additional examinations, they were broadly used to determine the presence of poor effort.

However, the development of stand-alone malingering measures gradually increased and became popular among clinicians and practitioners. Posterior findings suggested that EVI may have less sensitivity than stand-alone malingering measures, and subsequently, findings must be viewed in a broader context (Lange, Sullivan, & Anderson, 2005). Despite this, EVI are still considered of great utility in the clinical practice. *Table 1* presents some examples of embedded validity indicators, based on Boone (2011).

**Table 1** Examples of Embedded Validity Indicators (EVIs) from Different Standard Neuropsychological Tests. Adapted from Boone (2011).

| Embedded Validity Indicator | Cutoff | Sensitivity | Specificty | Reference |
|---|---|---|---|---|
| -WAIS-III Age-Corrected Scaled Score digit span (ACSS) | ≤5 | .42 | .93 | (Babikian, Boone, Lu, & Arnold, 2006) |
| -WAIS-III Reliable Digit Span (RDS) | ≤6 | .45 | .93 | |
| -WAIS-III Time scores for forward digit span (in seconds, to recite a 3-digit string) | >2" | .38 | .93 | |
| Rey Auditory Verbal Learning Test RAVLT Recognition Trial/Equation | | | | |
| -(RAVLT) Recognition | <10 | .67 | .90+ | (Boone, Lu, & Wen, 2005) |
| -(RAVLT) Recognition minus false positives | <8 | .64 | .90+ | |
| -(RAVLT) Recognition minus false positives + primacy recognition | ≤12 | .74 | .90+ | |
| Rey Osterrieth Effort Equation copy + [(recognition minus atypical false positive errors) x 3] | ≤47 | .76 | .82 ~ .91 | (Lu, Boone, Cozolino,& Mitchell, 2003) |
| WAIS-III Digit Symbol Recognition DSR Trial/Equation | | | | (Kim et al., 2010) |
| (ACSS) | ≤3 | .18 | .97 | |
| Raw score | ≤32 | .34 | .91 | |
| Recognition | ≤5 | .59 | .89 | |
| 180-degree rotations | ≥2 | .33 | .89 | |
| time | ≥72" | .49 | .89 | |
| Combination Score [(Digit Symbol ACSS + number of correctly recognized on recognition trial) x 10] - time | ≤57" | .80 | .89 | |

*3.2.2 Stand-alone Measures (Effort Measures)*

Different strategies have been specially developed to detect the presence of MND. These detection strategies, known as stand-alone measures or effort measures cover all cognitive domains but the majority mainly assesses memory functions. Since memory impairment is the most frequent cognitive complaint among traumatic brain injury (TBI) patients (Jones, Anderson, Cole, & Hathaway-Nepple, 1996), the detection of malingered memory impairment has been a particular focus of research (Barrash, Suhr, & Manzal, 2004). In (2000) Sweet, Condit, & Nelson, listed some EM with demonstrated utility for identifying feigned memory impairment. Among them we found the

Amsterdam Short-Term Memory Test (ASTM test; Schagen, Schmand, de Sterke, & Lindeboom, 1997), the Digit Memory Test (Vickery, Berry, Inman, Harris, & Orey, 2001), the Portland Digit Recognition Test (PDRT; Binder, 1993), the Test of Memory Malingering (TOMM; Tombaugh, 1996), the Word Memory Test (WMT; Green, 2005), and the Victoria Symptom Validity Test (VSVT; Slick, Hopp, Strauss, & Thompson, 1997). Effort measures are developed under different underlying principles. Rogers (2008) made a complete revision of the different existing detection strategies to determine poor effort (see Rogers, 2008). Some of them are: a) Magnitude of error, b) Performance curve, c) violation of learning principles, d) floor effect tests, e) atypical test pattern, f) symptom frequency, and g) symptom validity testing. However, among all detection strategies, symptom validity testing (SVT) is the most widely used in settings where some external incentives are present and malingering might occur (Grote & Hook, 2007). Therefore, the following section describes the SVT detection strategy.

## 3.3 Symptom Validity Testing (SVT)

### 3.3.1 General Description

Symptom Validity Testing (SVT) is based on the forced-choice method that was originally developed in the context of psychophysics (Macmillan & Creelman, 2008). SVT was initially implemented by Grosz and Zimmerman (1965) in an experimental analysis of hysterical blindness, and used a decade after by Pankratz, Fausti, and Peed (1975) in the context of malingering detection.

The rationale underlying SVT is simple. A previously defined number of forced-choice trials are presented to the examinee, where only one outcome per trial is possible: success or failure. Then, the amount of successfully answered trials that can be obtained by chance alone is estimated by using the binomial distribution. Usually, the normal approximation to the binomial has been applied. The final scores are calculated as follows (Siegel, 1956):

$$z = \frac{[(x_n \pm 0.5) - NP]}{\sqrt{NPQ}} \tag{1}$$

Where $x_n$ is the total score obtained by the examinee, $N$ is the number of forced-choice trials, $P$ is the probability of success and $Q$ is the probability of failure. The examinee's total score is simply the sum of all successfully answered trials. For a better approximation to the normal curve, a correction factor of 0.5 is added when the total score falls below the mean, and subtracted when it falls above the mean. Then, scores that fall significantly below the chance level "would seem to offer rather definitive evidence of an intentional (i.e., non-chance) attempt to perform poorly on the test by active avoidance of the correct response" (Grote & Hook, 2007, p.45).

This inference is feasible because most SVT are relatively easy, even for severe cognitive impaired patients (Morel & Shepherd, 2008; Slick et al., 2003). *Figure 2* shows an example of the binomial probability density function for a 20 trials two-alternative forced-choice task (2AFC).

### 3.3.2 The Sensitivity Problem of SVT

For many years, the standard approach in malingering assessment has been to achieve high specificity at the expense of sensitivity, in order to reduce the false positive rates (Iverson, 2007). On the one hand, this turns the below-chance criterion of SVT into a safe and reliable index of poor effort when results are positive. On the other hand, the inherent conservatism of the approach only allows for the identification of a small subset of malingerers (Beetar & Williams, 1995; Rogers, 2008; Slick et al., 2003). For instance,

Beetar & Williams (1995) pointed out that tests of symptom validity may not have enough sensitivity to detect milder forms of malingering.

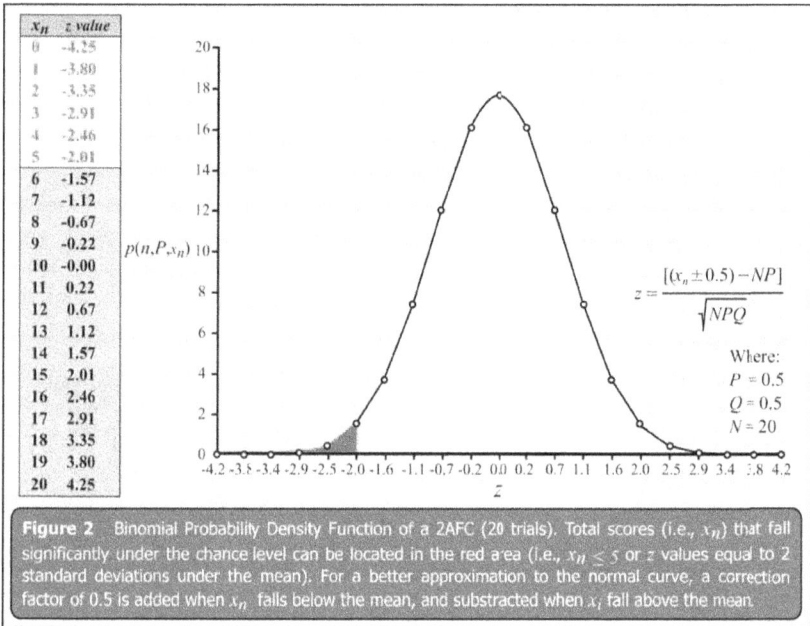

| $x_n$ | $z$ value |
|-----|-----|
| 0 | -4.25 |
| 1 | -3.80 |
| 2 | -3.35 |
| 3 | -2.91 |
| 4 | -2.46 |
| 5 | -2.01 |
| **6** | **-1.57** |
| **7** | **-1.12** |
| **8** | **-0.67** |
| **9** | **-0.22** |
| **10** | **-0.00** |
| **11** | **0.22** |
| **12** | **0.67** |
| **13** | **1.12** |
| **14** | **1.57** |
| **15** | **2.01** |
| **16** | **2.46** |
| **17** | **2.91** |
| **18** | **3.35** |
| **19** | **3.80** |
| **20** | **4.25** |

$$z = \frac{[(x_n \pm 0.5) - NP]}{\sqrt{NPQ}}$$

Where:
$P = 0.5$
$Q = 0.5$
$N = 20$

**Figure 2**  Binomial Probability Density Function of a 2AFC (20 trials). Total scores (i.e., $x_n$) that fall significantly under the chance level can be located in the red area (i.e., $x_n \leq 5$ or $z$ values equal to 2 standard deviations under the mean). For a better approximation to the normal curve, a correction factor of 0.5 is added when $x_n$ falls below the mean, and substracted when $x_i$ fall above the mean.

Slick and colleagues (2003) found that using the criterion of below-chance performance result in excellent specificity, but poor sensitivity. A more extreme assertion it has recently provided by Rogers (2008, p.25), who stated that SVT strategy "is typically successful in less than 25% of feigned cases".

In order to increase the low sensitivity of SVT, researchers working on test construction began to derive empirically cutoff scores (Iverson & Binder, 2000). Currently, many SVT (e.g., the Portland Digit Recognition Test [PDRT], Binder, 1993; the Test of Memory Malingering [TOMM], Tombaugh, 1996; the Validity Indicator Profile [VIP], Frederick, 1997; and the Word Memory Test [WMT], Green, 2005) do not use the below-chance criterion as the primary decision rule for the determination of poor effort

(Frederick & Speed, 2007). Although the use of empirically derived cutoff scores has some advantages, such as increasing sensitivity levels and diminishing false-negative rates, it may also introduce some difficulties. Firstly, when a test is used in different populations or settings, specific norms need to be obtained (American Educational Research Association, American Psychological Association, & National Council on Measurement in Education, 1999). Secondly, sensitivity and specificity are fixed properties of a test only as long as this is used with similar groups of people (Streiner, 2003). As a consequence, these indices must also be recalculated when the test is used in populations with different characteristics. Thirdly, further revisions must be made when the validity of test score interpretations is compromised by new research data, substantial changes in the domain of application, or new conditions of test use are recommended (American Educational Research Association et al., 1999). These arguments suggest that test norms and accuracy classification indices should be updated periodically, which generally entails a considerable spending of time, resources, and effort. In sum, the use of empirically derived norms improved SVT's sensitivity but also undermined its original purpose and main advantage that is to determine poor effort by simply using the below-chance criterion of SVT. Being aware of this problem, some researchers proposed the use of statistical measures such as odds and likelihood ratios, or Bayesian methods as strategies for effort assessment (Iverson, 2007; Millis, 2008).

In the next section the use of Bayesian inference is proposed, because it yields intuitive results and because it takes into account prior knowledge about malingering base rates and about commonalities and differences between individual participants. In addition, Bayesian methods do not necessarily require complex and time-consuming methods for the construction and validation of malingering instruments (Mossman, 2000). Finally, Bayesian methods allow automatic updating of knowledge as more information becomes available.

3.4 Bayesian Analysis: An Overview

*3.4.1 Fundamentals of Bayesian Analysis*

In statistics, there are two extensive categories of interpretations of Probability: frequentist inference and Bayesian inference. Frecuentist inference makes predictions about experiments whose outcomes depend basically upon random processes (Jeffreys, 1961). On the contrary, Bayesian inference is able to assign probabilities to any statement, even when a random process is not involved (O'Hagan, Forster, & Kendall, 1994). In a Bayesian framework, a probability is a way to embody an individual's degree of belief in a statement, or given some evidence.

A Bayesian analysis generally involves the updating of prior knowledge or information in light of newly available experimental data (Samaniego, 2010). This method combines three sources of information: a) A model that says how latent parameters generate data, b) the prior probability distribution, and c) the observed data (i.e., the likelihood). The prior distribution, denoted $p(\theta)$, represents our degree of uncertainty about the parameters of interest, and needs to be expressed as a probability distribution. This prior distribution may also reflect our degree of knowledge about the same parameters. Therefore, the more informative is our prior distribution, the less will be our degree of uncertainty about the parameters. The likelihood is given by the conditional probability distribution $p(D|\theta)$, as a function of $\theta$ for the observed data $D$. Bayes' rule specifies how the prior information $p(\theta)$ and the data – that is, the likelihood $p(D|\theta)$ – can be combined to arrive at the posterior distribution denoted $p(\theta|D)$:

$$p(\theta|D) = \frac{p(D|\theta)\,p(\theta)}{p(D)} \qquad (2.1)$$

This equation is often verbalized as:

$$\text{posterior} = \frac{\text{likelihood} \times \text{prior}}{\text{marginal likelihood}} \qquad (2.2)$$

Note that the probability of the observed data (i.e., the marginal likelihood) does not involve parameter $\theta$, and is given by a single number that ensures that the area under the posterior distribution equals 1 (Lee & Wagenmakers, 2013).

Therefore, equation 2.2 is often written as:

$$p(\theta|D) \propto p(D|\theta)\, p(\theta) \qquad (2.3)$$

Which says, "the posterior is proportional (i.e., $\propto$) to the likelihood times the prior".

Thus, the compromise between the likelihood and the prior distribution is achieved by the simple process of multiplying $p(D|\theta)$ by $p(\theta)$, at every value of $\theta$ (O'Hagan & Forster, 2004). Following the Bayes theorem, this combination produces the posterior probability distribution, which represents what has been learned from the data (see *Figure 3*).

One of the benefits of the Bayesian approach is that the prior (i.e., $p(\theta)$) moderates the influence provided by the data (i.e., $p(D|\theta)$). This compromise leads to less pessimism when data is unexpectedly bad and less optimism when it is unexpectedly good (O'Hagan et al., 1994). Both influences are beneficial, and help us to make more realistic inferences and take better decisions.

*3.4.2 Bayesian Analysis in Effort Assessment*

Paraphrasing decision theory we can roughly say that a good decision rule can be understood as a Bayes rule with respect to some given prior (Young & Smith, 2005). To determine whether or not someone is giving his or her best effort during testing can be also seen as a decision-making process. Usually, what makes decisions hard is uncertainty, and Bayesian methods can quantify those uncertainties using personal probabilities (O'Hagan & Forster, 2004). In a Bayesian framework, the quantification of uncertainty is a crucial factor to achieve rational and coherent evidence-based decisions.

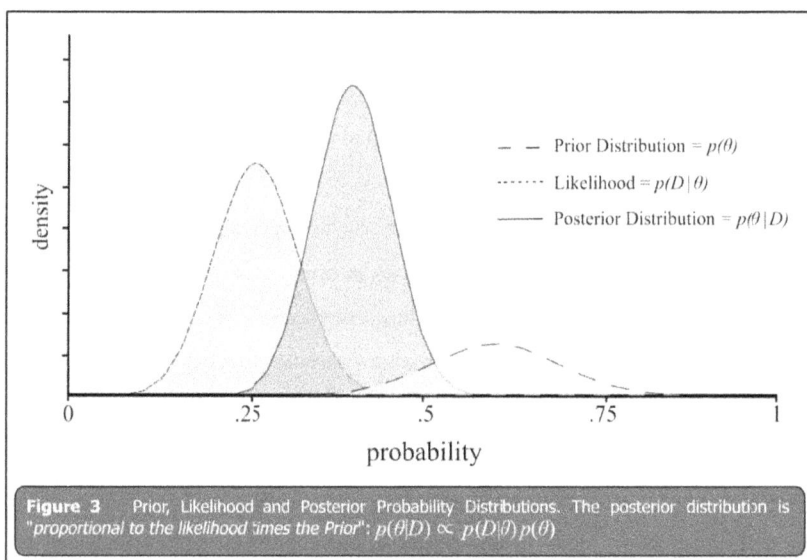

**Figure 3**    Prior, Likelihood and Posterior Probability Distributions. The posterior distribution is *"proportional to the likelihood times the Prior"*: $p(\theta|D) \propto p(D|\theta)\,p(\theta)$

According to Iverson (2007) Bayesian methods provide strong statistical evidence to underpin a clinical inference regarding where a person falls along the spectrum of the level of effort during testing. Since malingering can be better described as a continuum rather than a discrete taxonomy (Walters et al., 2008) it might be better to conceptualize effort through probabilistic estimations instead of simple dichotomous terms (Iverson, 2007).

Mossman and Hart (1996) used a Bayesian approach for estimating the level of effort displayed by examinees. In their study, Mossman and Hart (1996) re-analyzed data from previously published malingering studies. Results allowed for a precise estimation of the probability that an examinee is feigning some cognitive or emotional impairment (Mossman & Hart, 1996). However, Rogers and Salekin (1998) discouraged the use of the Bayesian approach for effort testing. The main reason for this was the existence of high variability in the base rates of malingering. Rogers and Salekin (1998) argued that an implicit assumption of Bayes' theorem is that the base rate of a specific condition (e.g., malingering) is measurable and relatively stable. The available evidence showed, however, that malingering base rates were highly variable (Rogers, Sewell, & Goldstein, 1994; Rogers, Salekin, Sewell, Goldstein, & Leonard, 1998).

Based on the previous idea, Rogers and Salekin (1998) suggested that a Bayesian approach had little clinical utility in assessing effort in the context of malingering. In recent years, the increase in malingering research has yielded key information about malingering base rates (Larrabee, 2007). A survey study of neuropsychologists involved in forensic work showed a base rate of 30% in persons alleging personal injury, disability, and chronic pain (Mittenberg, Patton, Canyock, & Condit, 2002). The same study also found that the highest base rate of malingering was 38.5% in litigants alleging mild head injury (Mittenberg et al., 2002). Another review encompassing 1,363 mild traumatic brain-injury litigants reports a base rate of 40% for malingering (Larrabee, 2003). Miller, Boyd, Cohn, Wilson, and McFarland (2006) found that 54% of Social Security disability applicants failed in two effort measures. Later, Larrabee (2007) estimated that base rates of malingering approach or exceed 50% for a range of civil and criminal settings.

The updated knowledge about malingering base rates shows values that are subject to less variability than surmised before. This knowledge allows us to propose more specific and informative priors on malingering base rates than a decade ago. In addition, the emergence of modern Bayesian methods for making inferences using more sophisticated hierarchical models allows the possibility of estimating malingering base rates from the observed data. Together, these empirical and methodological advances address the initial concerns about the appropriateness of Bayesian methods raised by Rogers and Salekin (1998).

### 3.4.3 The Model: A Bayesian Latent Group Analysis

The goal of our Bayesian latent group analysis is to identify participants who are displaying poor effort when tested. This Bayesian approach quantifies the confidence with which each participant $i$ is classified, and also estimates base rates of malingering from the observed data.

Firstly, model specifications assume the existence of two latent groups: a) the bona fide (i.e., honest response) and b) the malingering group (i.e., feigned cognitive impairment). The former corresponds to participants who answer the test giving their best, and the latter corresponds to participants who are instructed to perform poorly by feigning cognitive impairment during testing. Secondly, the model assumes that the bona fide group has an unknown mean rate $\mu_{bon}$ of answering any particular test item correctly. The mean rate $\mu_{bon}$ is higher than chance (i.e., $.5 < \mu_{bon} < 1$). A third assumption of the model is that the malingering group has an unknown mean rate $\mu_{mal}$ of answering any question correctly, and that $\mu_{bon}$ is greater than $\mu_{mal}$ (or, equivalently, that $\mu_{mal} = \mu_{bon} - \mu_{diff}$, with $\mu_{diff} > 0$). Together, these three assumptions simply state that bona fide participants have a higher success rate than malingerers.

Fourthly, our Bayesian approach assumes that participants within each group are similar to each other, but not identical. This psychologically plausible assumption is implemented through a hierarchical structure, where individual parameter estimates $\theta_i$ are constrained by group-level distributions (Nilsson, Rieskamp, & Wagenmakers, 2010; Shiffrin, Lee, Kim, & Wagenmakers, 2008; Lee, 2010). We use a standard "Beta-binomial" hierarchical model, in which each individual's success rate is constrained by a group-level Beta distribution. We consider a parameterization in which the $\alpha$ and $\beta$ parameters from the Beta($\alpha$, $\beta$) distribution are transformed into a group mean $\mu = \alpha/(\alpha + \beta)$ and a group precision $\lambda = \alpha + \beta$. For participants in the bona fide group, individual success rates are assumed to be governed by a group-level Beta distribution with mean $\mu_{bon}$ and precision $\lambda_{bon}$; for participants in the malingering group, the group-level Beta distribution has mean $\mu_{mal}$ and precision $\lambda_{mal}$. Within each group, the similarity of its members is quantified by the precision $\lambda$. When $\lambda$ is high, the group members perform similarly, and when $\lambda$ is low, the group members perform differently.

Figure 4 represents the structure of our Bayesian latent group analysis of malingering in graphical model notation. Nodes indicate data or variables, and arrows indicate statistical dependencies. In Figure 4, nodes $n$ (i.e., the total number of trials) and $k_i$ (i.e., the number of correct answers for each participant $i$, the maximum of which depends on $n$) are shaded, indicating that these variables have been observed. These nodes are also square, indicating that they represent discrete as opposed to continuous values. The plate indicates a structure that is repeated (in this case, it is repeated once for every participant). The node $\varphi$ represents the prior assumption about the malingering base rate.

The binary variable $z$ determines group membership; based on $z_i$, the individual success rate parameter $\varphi_i$ is constrained either by the group-level distribution for the malingerers (i.e., a Beta distribution with mean $\mu_{mal}$ and precision $\lambda_{mal}$) or by a group-level distribution for the bona fide participants (i.e., a Beta distribution with mean $\mu_{bon}$ and precision $\lambda_{bon}$). In the graphical model, $\mu_{mal}$ is deterministically calculated as $logit(\mu_{mal}) = logit(\mu_{bon}) - \mu_{diff}$, which is why node $\mu_{mal}$ has double borders.

*3.4.3.1 Priors on Malingering Base Rates.*

The prior distribution over parameters "captures our initial assumptions or state of knowledge about the psychological variables they represent" (Lee & Wagenmakers, 2013, p.45). The present model can incorporate different prior information about base rates of malingering, and can even estimate these base rates from data. In the graphical model shown in *Figure 4*, this information is encoded in the prior for the classification variable $z$. Specifically, for each participant $i$, the classification variable has a prior that reflects, or can reflect, advance knowledge about base rates. Thus, $z_i$ has a Bernoulli prior $\varphi$, and our model explores two ways to deal with the uncertainty in this prior.

The first way is assigning $\varphi$ itself a prior distribution such that it can be estimated from the data. Here, we assigned $\varphi$ a Beta(5,5) prior, which is relatively uninformative but does not assign a lot of mass to the extremes of the scale. This reflects a prior belief that we are mostly uncertain about the true rate of malingering, but do not believe it to be very low (e.g., 5%) or very high (e.g., 95%).

The second method is essentially a robustness analysis, in which we implemented this Bayesian approach with three different prior beliefs about the base rate of malingering (e.g., $\varphi = .5$; $\varphi = .4$; and $\varphi = .3$. These priors cover the plausible range of values for malingering base rates according to the cited literature. If we find that our analyses give essentially the same answers for all these base-rate choices, we can conclude that the data are informative enough that the exact assumptions made about base rates do not matter. On the other hand, if our analyses are different, we have to conclude that data are more ambiguous, and more work is needed to quantify the prior beliefs for the base rate.

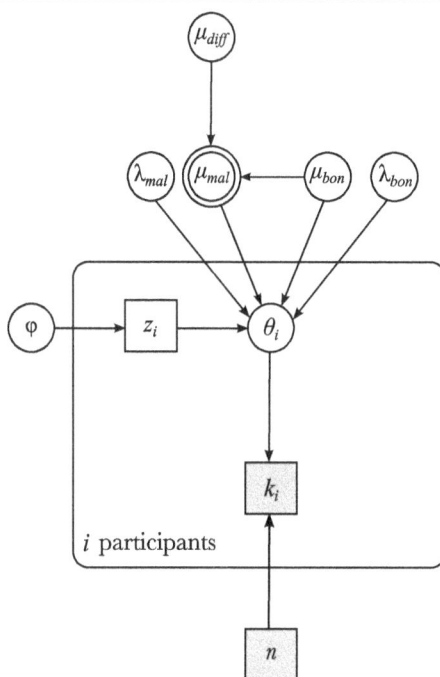

**Figure 4** Graphical model for inferring membership of two latent groups. One group consists of malingerers and the other consists of bona fide participants. Each participant has their own rate of answering test questions correctly, albeit one that is constrained by a group level distribution.
Source: Ortega, A., Wagenmakers, E.-J., Lee. M.D., Markowitsch, H.J., & Piefke, M. (2012). A Bayesian latent group analysis for detecting poor effort in the assessment of malingering . Archives of Clinical Neuropsychology, 27, 453-465.

*3.4.3.2 Markov chain Monte Carlo Sampling Method.*

Because the posterior distributions in our Bayesian approach are analytically intractable, we implemented the model using Markov chain Monte Carlo sampling method (MCMC; e.g., Gamerman and Lopes, 2006; Gilks, Richardson, & Spiegelhalter, 1996). MCMC sampling is a numerical method that repeatedly draws values from a posterior distribution in order to approximate it to any desired degree of accuracy. "Sampling" means drawing a set of values, so that the relative likelihood that any particular value will be selected is proportional to the density of the posterior distribution at that value. Then, if we have a sufficiently large sample from any distribution, then we can effectively have almost the whole distribution in front of us, and anything we want to know about the distribution can be calculated from the sample (O'Hagan & Forster, 2004). Hence, what MCMC does is randomly drawing a very large simulated sample from the posterior distribution and, in this way, accurately estimate which are the most probable values for the parameters of interest (e.g., $\varphi$).

The WinBUGS software program (Lunn, Spiegelhalter, Thomas, & Best, 2009; Lunn, Thomas, Best, & Spiegelhalter, 2000) uses both the model file and the data to conduct the MCMC sampling, and outputs the results (i.e., approximations to the posterior distributions, see *Figure 5*). Posterior distributions that are relatively peaked indicate relatively precise knowledge, whereas posterior distributions that are relatively flat indicate that knowledge is vague or uncertain. For more detailed information about Bayesian inference, see, for instance, O'Hagan and Forster (2004), Kruschke and John (2010), Lee and Wagenmakers (2010), and Dienes (2011).

*3.4.3.3 Model Summary.*

There are four main interesting features of this Bayesian approach. The first one is that the model learns from participants' answers and, in this way, estimates base rates from the data. This constitutes an important advantage and addresses the base rate problem raised by Rogers and Salekin (1998).

The second one is the use of a hierarchical model, which has the advantage of being able to account simultaneously for both differences and similarities between participants (e.g., Nilsson et al., 2010). Since individual parameters $\theta_i$ originate from a group-level distribution, participants are not treated as if their answers were completely independent from the others. This group-level constraint helps avoiding the potentially unreliable estimation of a particular individual's parameter by borrowing strength of the information that is obtained from the other individuals (Nilsson et al., 2010). This makes the individual parameter estimates more reliable, because it incorporates more information into their inference. To the best of our knowledge, this approach has not been used before for helping in malingering detection.

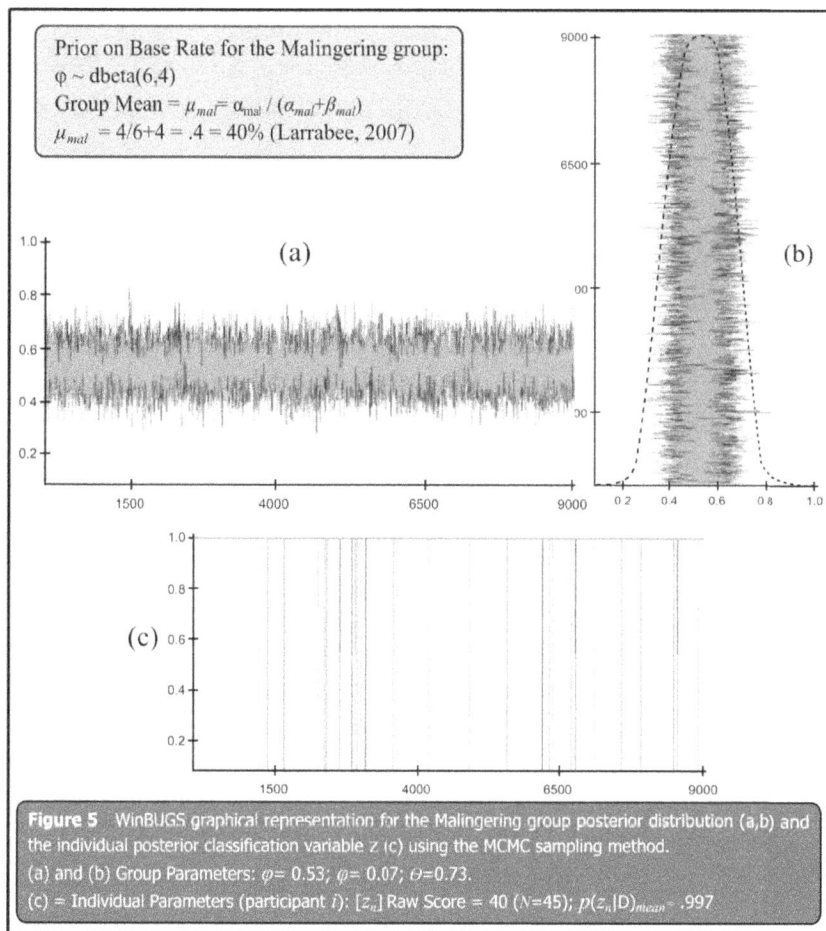

Prior on Base Rate for the Malingering group:
$\varphi \sim$ dbeta(6,4)
Group Mean $= \mu_{mal} = \alpha_{mal} / (\alpha_{mal} + \beta_{mal})$
$\mu_{mal} = 4/6+4 = .4 = 40\%$ (Larrabee, 2007)

**Figure 5** WinBUGS graphical representation for the Malingering group posterior distribution (a,b) and the individual posterior classification variable z (c) using the MCMC sampling method.
(a) and (b) Group Parameters: $\varphi = 0.53$; $\varphi = 0.07$; $\theta = 0.73$.
(c) = Individual Parameters (participant $i$): $[z_n]$ Raw Score = 40 ($N$=45); $p(z_n|D)_{mean} = .997$

A third advantage is that Bayesian methods apply equally validly to any sample size no matter how small this is. (e.g., Jaynes, 2003; Jeffreys, 1961). This makes Bayesian analysis especially well suited in research fields where participants need to meet very specific characteristics and, therefore, are rather scarce.

Finally, the Bayesian model allows us to quantify the certainty or confidence of the classification by means of a probability; for each subject $i$, this certainty is given by the posterior mean of the classification variable $z_i$. For instance, suppose the posterior mean of $z_8$ equals .01, and that of $z_{29}$ equals .43; this indicates that there is a 1% chance that Participant 8 belongs to the group of malingerers, and a 43% chance that Participant 29 belongs to the group of malingerers. Even though one may classify both participants as bona fide, the classification variable indicates that Participant 29 may need to undergo additional testing.

# 4 EMPIRICAL STUDIES

The present work is aimed at providing evidence that supports the utility of a Bayesian latent group analysis to determine the presence of poor effort in the context of malingering assessment. In particular, we investigated:

(i) The utility of a Bayesian latent group analysis to identify participants who displayed poor effort during neuropsychological testing using a simulation research design (Empirical *Study 1* and *2*)

(ii) The accuracy of a Bayesian approach compared to that of the SVT below-chance criterion (Empirical *Study 1*)

(iii) The utility of a Bayesian latent group analysis to differentiate between "coached" healthy participants who displayed poor effort and Neurological patients who performed at their best during neuropsychological testing (Empirical *Study 1*)

(iv) The diagnostic accuracy of the Bayesian latent group model, using the raw scores from a standard visual recognition forced-choice task (2AFC), the Test of Memory Malingering (TOMM; Tombaugh, 1996), and the Word Memory Test (WMT; Green, 2005), (Empirical *Study 2*)

(v) The utility of a Bayesian latent group analysis to identify participants who displayed poor effort during neuropsychological testing using a simulation research design in a sample of cognitively impaired patients (Empirical *Study 3*)

(vi) The stability of Bayesian effort estimates across different priors about malingering base rates (Empirical *Study 3*)

The following sections briefly describe the main findings and significance of our empirical studies. All studies used the same Bayesian latent group model. Bayesian analyses implemented a MCMC sampling method (e.g., Gamerman and Lopes, 2006), using the WinBUGS software program (Lunn et al., 2009). Further and detailed information about the model, methodological aspects, data analysis and results can be found in Ortega et al., 2012; Ortega, Labrenz, Markowitsch & Piefke, 2013 and Ortega, Piefke & Markowitsch, 2014.

4.1 Empirical Study 1

Ortega, A., Wagenmakers, E.-J., Lee, M. D., Markowitsch, H. J., & Piefke, M. (2012). A Bayesian latent group analysis for detecting poor effort in the assessment of malingering. *Archives of Clinical Neuropsychology, 27*, 453-465.

In *Study 1* we outline a novel Bayesian Latent Group Analysis whose goal is to identify participants displaying poor effort during neuropsychological assessment (see subsection *3.4.3*). This preliminary study encompassed two experiments.

    *Experiment 1* aimed at comparing the accuracy of our Bayesian model to that of the below-chance criterion used by symptom validity testing (SVT) as a strategy determine the presence of poor effort (see subsection *3.3.1*). Using a simulation research design, participants that performed at their best during testing (i.e., bona fide group) were differentiated from those instructed to feign some degree of cognitive impairment while being assessed (i.e., malingering group). In *Experiment 1*, malingering group participants were naive about how to simulate cognitive impairment during effort testing.

    *Experiment 2* also compared the accuracy of both detection strategies. However, neurological patients had to be differentiated from participants that were especially trained about how to feign cognitive impairment during testing (i.e., coached malingerering group). This modification is aimed at providing more external validity to our findings.

    Results of *Experiment 1* showed that the Bayesian Latent Group model accurately identified all participants. That is, the Bayesian model showed both 100% sensitivity and specificity. Using the SVT below-chance criterion sensitivity levels showed an important decrement to 20%. Despite this, the SVT below-chance criterion showed excellent specificity (100%). Results of *Experiment 2* also showed both 100% sensitivity and specificity for the Bayesian model when distinguishing between coached malingering participants and neurological patients. Using the SVT below-chance criterion none of the coached malingering participants was properly identified. This is, the SVT below-chance criterion was insensitive to detect poor effort. We may attribute this lack of sensitivity to the specific training that malingering group participants obtained to face the effort test. Despite this, and as in *Experiment 1*, specificity of the SVT below-chance criterion was 100%. That means that none of the neurological patients was misclassified as malingerer (i.e., false positives).

In both experiments, sensitivity levels were high for the Bayesian method, but low for the below-chance criterion of SVT. Additionally, the Bayesian approach proves to be resistant to possible effects of coaching. In conclusion, our Bayesian latent group model showed high classification accuracy when assessing poor effort and may complement existing methods for malingering determination.

## 4.2 Empirical Study 2

Ortega, A., Labrenz, S., Markowitsch, H. J., & Piefke, M. (2013). Diagnostic accuracy of a Bayesian latent group analysis for the detection of malingering-related poor effort. *The Clinical Neuropsychologist, 27,* 1019-1042.

Our previous study showed preliminary evidence that a Bayesian latent group model may help to optimize classification accuracy using a simulation research design. The present study is aimed at further evaluating the diagnostic accuracy of the Bayesian latent group model. To validate our Bayesian model, all participants were evaluated using a visual recognition forced-choice task (2AFC) and two known and well-validated SVT (i.e., Test of Memory Malingering [TOMM, Trial 2], Tommbaugh & Tombaugh, 1996; Word Memory Test [WMT, primary effort subtests], Green, 2005). All raw scores were analyzed using a Bayesian latent group model. Additionally, we report sensitivity, specificity, and predictive values because they are the most relevant classification accuracy indices in malingering research (Etherton, Bianchini, Ciota, Heinly, & Greve, 2006). We also reported the overall discrimination accuracy of the Bayesian model for each effort measure (i.e., 2AFC, TOMM, WMT). This study included two analyses.

Firstly, we evaluated the accuracy of a Bayesian model using a traditional simulation research design. The groups were called honest response (HR) and experimental malingering (EM), respectively. This analysis was conducted to corroborate previous findings using a Bayesian model to detect poor effort (Ortega, A., Wagenmakers, E.-J., Lee, M. D., Markowitsch, H. J., & Piefke, M., 2012). Secondly, we tested the accuracy of our model in the differentiation between patients who had real cognitive deficits (i.e., cognitively impaired group, CI) and participants who belonged to the EM group.

First analysis showed 100% accuracy for the Bayesian model in distinguishing between HR and EM participants, regardless of the effort measure. Second analysis successfully distinguished between CI patients and EM participants when estimates were obtained from the 2AFC and the TOMM raw scores. In this case the overall diagnostic accuracy can be evaluated as outstanding, according to Hosmer & Lemeshow criteria (2000). Nevertheless, diagnostic accuracy of the Bayesian model diminished when using the WMT total raw scores. The most plausible explanation for his decrement is the low performance in verbal recognition and fluency tasks observed in some patients of the CI group (see Ortega et al., 2013).

In sum, *Study 2* provides diagnostic accuracy indices that support the excellent classification accuracy of the Bayesian model to detect poor effort (see *Table 2*).

**Table 2** Classification accuracy of the Bayesian Model using the 2AFC visual recognition task, the Test of Memory Malingering (Trial 2), and the Word Memory Test (primary effort subscales). Adapted from Ortega, A., Labrenz, S., Markowitsch, H.J., & Piefke, M. (2013).

| | Classification accuracy indices | | |
|---|---|---|---|
| | 2AFC (raw scores) | TOMM Trial 2 (raw scores) | WMT primary effort subscales (raw scores) |
| Index | Value  95% CI | Value  95% CI | Value  95% CI |
| AUC[a] | .95  (.87 - 1) | .95  (.87 - 1) | .85  (.72 - .97) |
| Sensitivity | .95  (.75 - .99) | .95  (.75 - .99) | .95  (.75 - .99) |
| Specificity | .95  (.75 - .99) | .95  (.75 - .99) | .75  (.51 - .91) |
| LR (+) | 19 (2.81 - 128.7) | 19 (2.81 - 128.7) | 3.80 (1.77 - 8.17) |
| LR (−) | 0.05 (0.01 - 0.36) | 0.05 (0.01 - 0.36) | 0.07 (0.01 - 0.46) |
| PPV[b] | .93  (.90 - .94) | .93  (.90 - .94) | .72  (.68 - .75) |
| NPV[b] | .97  (.95 - .98) | .97  (.95 - .98) | .96  (.94 - .97) |

Note: AUC= Area Under the Curve; LR(+)= Likelihood Ratio for a positive test result; LR(−)= Likelihood Ratio for a negative test result; PPV= Positive Predictive Value; NPV: Negative Predictive Value.
a. Hosmer and Lemeshow (2000) guidelines were considered to interpret the AUC value.
b. PPV and NPV were estimated considering a malingering base rate of 40% (Larrabee, 2003, 2007; Larrabee et al., 2009).

## 4.3 Empirical Study 3

Ortega, A., Piefke, M., & Markowitsch, H. J. (2014). A Bayesian latent group analysis for detecting poor effort in a sample of cognitively impaired patients. *Journal of Clinical and Experimental Neuropsychology*, 36, 659-667.

*Study 1* and *Study 2* show high classification accuracy for a Bayesian latent group model using simulation research designs. Similarly, both studies evaluated the accuracy of the Bayesian model by differentiating between healthy participants (e.g., coached malingerers, experimental malingerers) and neurological patients (e.g., stroke, TBI). *Study 3* aimed at further evaluating the utility of a Bayesian latent group analysis for identifying participants who displayed poor effort during neuropsychological testing in a sample of cognitively impaired patients. Including only patients with some degree of cognitive impairment it allows for a better extrapolation of results to more realistic settings and for increasing the external validity of the findings. As in our previous studies, patients were randomly assigned to both an honest responding group (HR) and to a symptom exaggeration group (SE). As previously mentioned, prior information about base rates exerts some influence on the individual posterior classification estimates of effort or $p(z_i \mid D)$. Both studies 1 and 2, assumed a prior about malingering base rate equal to 40% (Larrabee, 2003, 2007; Larrabee et al., 2008). A base rate of 40% is commonly accepted among malingering researchers (Ortega et al., 2012). However, patients with cognitive impairment rarely score lower than chance level (i.e., <50% correct answers) in SVT measures (Loring, Larrabee, Lee, & Meador, 2007). Moreover, some studies reported low malingering base rates within non-litigant medical patients (Mittemberg et al., 2002; Sullivan, Lange, & Dawes, 2005). Considering the characteristics of the present sample, a malingering base rate of 8% was assumed to conduct the *main analysis* of *Study 3*.

Nevertheless, the accuracy of any prediction model may vary according to the base rate of the condition in any given setting (Rosenfeld, Sands, & Van Gorp, 2000).

Therefore, we performed additional analysis to observe the stability of Bayesian effort estimates across different priors about malingering base rates.

*Main analysis* showed 90% sensitivity and 100% specificity. We also observed a high overall diagnostic accuracy for the Bayesian model (AUC=.95). These results can be considered as positive. *Additional analysis* reveals interesting results. Within the HR group, variations on $p(z_i \mid D)$ mean values were subtle, and did not affect classification accuracy. On the contrary, within the SE group important variations can be observed in some patient's $p(z_i \mid D)$ mean values. These variations affected sensitivity but not specificity. Furthermore, higher variations were observed in the case of examinees that scored in the range between "above chance" (i.e., > 50% correct answers) and "below the cutoff score" (i.e., near-pass scores; see Bigler, 2012). Results of the *additional analysis* highlight the importance of considering information about malingering base rates in effort assessment (see Ortega et al., 2014). The previous idea is further discussed in the Concluding Discussion section.

# 5  CONCLUDING DISCUSSION

Findings of the empirical research, conducted in the context of the present doctoral thesis, have been previously discussed in the respective scientific manuscripts (see Ortega et al., 2012, 2013, 2014). However, main findings and some relevant issues are further discussed to provide a concluding view of why using Bayesian approaches in neuropsychological evaluation and, particularly, in effort assessment.

## 5.1 Classification Accuracy of a Bayesian Latent Group Analysis in Effort Assessment

In three studies, classification accuracy of the Bayesian latent group model has been investigated. Overall findings suggest high classification accuracy of the Bayesian model when assessing for poor effort. For instance, in *Study 1* the Bayesian model accurately distinguished healthy participants who feigned cognitive impairment from those who performed at their best (i.e., 100% sensitivity, 100% specificity). This preliminary finding is in agreement with previous studies using Bayesian approaches (e.g., Mossman & Hart, 1996). It also provided first evidence of the potential utility of the Bayesian latent group model in effort assessment. However, simulation designs have lower external validity than other designs used in malingering research (e.g., known-groups comparison; see Rogers, 2008). To increase external validity, *Study 1* included two new groups: a) a stroke and TBI patients group and b) a group of participants who received special training about how feigning cognitive impairment during testing (i.e., coached malingerers). Results showed again 100% sensitivity and specificity. This finding suggests that the Bayesian model may be resistant to coaching (see Ortega et al., 2012). The phenomenon of coaching is being increasingly investigated (Dunn, Shear, Howe, & Ris, 2003; Brennan, et al., 2009). Hence, the evidence provided by *Study 1* might encourage researchers in this area to including Bayesian models for coaching detection in effort assessment. This suggestion might be particularly interesting when considering that traditional SVT are not robust against coaching (Gunstad, & Suhr, 2001; Verschuere, Meijer, & Crombez, 2008).

Another interesting finding of *Study 1* is that classification accuracy of the Bayesian model was higher than the traditional SVT below chance-criterion. Particularly, sensitivity levels were superior when using a Bayesian approach. The observed difference that favored the Bayesian model was even greater when the clinical and the coached group were included. This finding is in absolute agreement with those studies that previously criticized the low sensitivity levels of the SVT below-chance criterion (Beetar & Williams, 1995; Rogers, 2008; Slick et al., 2003). However, both approaches showed excellent specificity (i.e., no false negative results). These preliminary findings provided first evidence that suggest that a Bayesian model may serve as complement to the existing techniques (e.g., SVT) to determine poor effort.

As observed in *Study 1*, findings of *Study 2* suggest high diagnostic accuracy of the Bayesian model; even using raw scores from two SVT (i.e., TOMM, WMT). Using raw scores from two standardized and widespread SVT allowed validating the utility of the Bayesian model. This finding of *Study 2* might encourage interested researchers to re-examine their data sets using this Bayesian model. Overall diagnostic accuracy indices were obtained (see *Table 2*). Results showed outstanding overall classification accuracy levels when estimates were obtained from both the 2AFC and the TOMM. However, sensitivity levels decreased when estimates were obtained from the WMT. A feasible explanation for this finding is that, as observed, low performance in verbal tasks might affect performance in the WMT; however, this should be further investigated. A more detailed discussion is provided in the manuscript (see Ortega et al., 2013).

Including only cognitively impaired patients increased the external validity of *Study 3*. This allows extrapolating the impact of the previous studies to more genuine settings. Results showed again excellent overall diagnostic accuracy levels (see Ortega et al., 2014). Despite the excellent results observed, it is still necessary to conduct further research and provide more evidence of the benefits of Bayesian models in effort assessment.

A common finding across all studies was the excellent specificity of the Bayesian latent group model. Since the standard approach in malingering assessment is achieving high specificity at the expense of sensitivity (Iverson, 2007), this finding should be considered as very important. Avoiding the presence of false positive results, and its potential harmful consequences on examinees, should be a key point in every effort assessment method. Results of all three studies suggest that including Bayesian models in applied settings (e.g., clinical, medico-legal, research, forensic) may be of high interest and utility.

## 5.2 Individual Posterior Classification Estimates of Effort

As recently mentioned, providing probabilistic estimates of effort is of particular interest. Individual posterior classification estimates, $p(z_i \mid D)$ mean values, represent the level of effort displayed by an examinee during testing. These $p(z_i \mid D)$ mean values can also be seen as the degree of certainty that we have on each examinee classification (Ortega et al., 2012). To the best of our knowledge, no current effort assessment methods provide this individual posterior classification estimate of effort. This feature of the Bayesian model can be seen as an advantage with respect to traditional effort measures (e.g., SVT).

Several authors recommended interpreting effort as a continuum rather than taxonomy (Iverson, 2010, Walters et al., 2008; Walters, Berry, Lanyon, & Murphy, 2009). From this view, effort could be better seen as a variable that increases or decreases in magnitude but not as a discrete variable. This perspective raises an important issue about the way in which effort should be evaluated. As a continuous variable, instead of dichotomous variable, a probabilistic approach may better estimate the level at which the examinee's performance could be. Iverson (2010) recently presented and described a "Continuum of effort" which ranges from "definite poor effort" to "exceptional effort" (p.110). Clinically estimating at which point of this continuum an examinee's performance is, seems to be extremely difficult if not impossible. Then, probabilistic estimates may constitute more accurate and precise indices of the levels of effort displayed by an examinee. They may also better capture and reflect the nature of effort.

Bigler (2012) recently proposed an important remark about the way in which effort is determined. In an exhaustive review on "SVT, effort and neuropsychological assessment", Bigler criticized the issue of using cutoff scores in neuropsychological testing. The use of cutoff scores assumes the existence of delimited categories that can be mutually excluded depending on the results of a test. Usually a cutoff score helps the clinician to determine in which category the examinee should be classified. However, in Bigler's (2012) opinion, cutoff scores represent artificial "pass-fail" dichotomies and inherently result in some misclassification (i.e., false positives, false negatives). Moreover, the risk of misclassification is particularly high in those scores that are slightly over or under the cutoff (i.e., near-pass scores).

In sum, both a) considering effort as a continuum that varies in magnitude, and b) providing more accurate probabilistic estimates of effort may help diminishing the risk of misclassification. In Iverson's (2007) words: "...Clinicians are encouraged to conceptualize poor effort during testing, and exaggerated symptom reporting, not in simple dichotomous terms, but through probabilistic estimations. Bayesian methods provide strong statistical evidence to underpin a clinical inference regarding where a person falls along the spectrum of the accuracy of symptom reporting and the level of effort on testing."(p.98). From this view, a Bayesian latent group model provides the clinician accurate and precise $p(z_i \mid D)$ mean values that may definitely improve decision-making processes in effort determination. At least, the evidence provided in the present three studies supports this hypothesis.

5.3 Including Malingering Base Rates for Effort Assessment


In 2000, Rosenfeld et al. highlighted the importance of considering base rates in effort assessment. The influence of base rates on the accuracy of any predictive method (e.g., diagnostic) has been also previously stipulated (Grove, 2005; Mossman, 2000; Streiner, 2003). Rosenfeld et al. (2000) stated, "The accuracy of prediction models varies tremendously according to the base rate of the condition being predicted in any given setting" (p.352). Since every Bayesian approach includes prior information about base rates, it is especially well suited for effort assessment. Streiner (2003) asserts that when prevalence rates are low, a test is best used to rule out a condition. On the other hand, when prevalence rates are high any test is best used to rule in a condition. Finally, the optimal scenario to better predict any condition is when base rate is exactly 50% (Streiner, 2003). If we accurately follow Streiner's (2003) arguments, base rates of a condition will affect some classification accuracy estimates. For instance, both Positive Predictive Value (PPP) and Negative Predictive Value (NPP) are affected by base rates (Streiner, 2003).

The proposed Bayesian latent group model incorporates prior information about malingering base rates. By this way, individual posterior classification estimates are obtained considering information about the base rate associated to any particular evaluation setting (e.g., non-litigant medical or psychiatric, litigant mild cognitive impairment, social security disability claimants). For example, in non-litigant medical or psychiatric settings malingering base rates tend to be lower than in litigant patients seeking for compensation (e.g., medical leave, economical compensation from health insurance companies). Individual posterior classification effort estimates (or any other index that is affected by prevalence) may vary depending on the assumed prior on malingering base rate (see Ortega et al., 2014). More importantly, when prior information about base rates is not incorporated in any kind of analysis, it is implicitly (and falsely) assumed that the base rate equals 50%. The immediate consequence is to underestimate examinees' efforts level when base rates are lower than 50%, and to overestimate them when base rates are higher than 50%. This would lead to obtain inaccurate effort levels that may also led to misclassification. Even worse, this inaccuracy will not equally affect all examinees. Results of *Study 3* suggest that higher variations on individual posterior classification estimates occur in the range of near-pass scores, increasing the risk of misclassification (see Ortega et al., 2014).

Unfortunately, considerations about the importance of including malingering base rates when assessing effort have not received enough attention. In the same line, Iverson (2007) stated, "...This is a critical issue. Over the past several years, researchers have been encouraging the use of Bayesian methods for effort testing. Unfortunately, Bayesian methods, and other interesting statistical methodologies, including odds and likelihood ratios, are rarely used in mainstream clinical practice." (p.97).

5.4 Clinical Relevance, Limitations and Further Directions

Consequences of misclassification in clinical assessment are numerous and potentially harmful. On the one hand, false positive errors may lead to improperly designating persons as "malingerers" and, subsequently, result in failure to administer needed treatment, wrongful withdrawal of social entitlements, or erroneous legal decisions (Mossman, Wygant, & Gervais, 2012). On the other hand, false negative errors (i.e., failing to detect feigned problems) can lead to incorrect legal determinations (e.g., finding of incompetence to stand trial) or the institution of treatment that is inappropriate and potentially damaging (Mosman et al., 2012).

To avoid or, at least, minimize the risk of misclassification in effort assessment the emphasis should be put into providing clinicians accurate and precise methods. According to Barrash et al. (2004) the necessity for reliable methods to evaluate effort is permanent. The present studies propose a Bayesian latent group analysis model that offers reliable and accurate estimates of effort. In particular, Bayesian individual posterior classification probabilities, $p(z_i \mid D)$, provide complementary information to interpret an examinee's performance and thus help clinicians to avoid committing false positives and false negative errors. Using Bayesian individual posterior classification probabilities may improve clinician's decision-making processes in effort determination. The latter may have direct implications in effort determination and, therefore, becomes clinically relevant. Despite, we do not promote our Bayesian latent group model as the one and only method for determining poor effort. Instead, we suggest that the proposed Bayesian model complements the information provided by the existing methods in useful ways. This synergy of methods may enrich the evaluation process and yield more coherent diagnoses of malingering.

Despite the positive results observed across all three studies, there are two main limitations that should be mentioned. The first one is related to small sample sizes used in the present studies. Even though is well documented that Bayesian methods can be applied in small samples (Jeffreys, 1961; Jaynes, 2003), it must be noted that classification accuracy indices (i.e., sensitivity and specificity) will most likely decrease upon cross-validation when using larger samples. This can be considered as a limitation of our studies. Additionally, it needs to be considered that variations in the base rates may also affect classification accuracy indices (Streiner, 2003). Nevertheless, using Bayesian models are especially well suited when participants need to meet very specific characteristics and, therefore, are rather scarce (Ortega et al., 2012). A second main limitation of the present studies is related to the contexts where participants and patients were recruited. According to the format of simulation research designs, healthy participants were instructed to feign cognitive impairment whereas others were asked to honestly answering the tests. The main limitation of using this kind of designs is the difficulty of generalizing results to more realistic settings (Rogers, 2008). To improve this drawback, patients with real cognitive impairments after stroke, TBI or other medical etiologies were recruited. Nonetheless, the presence of external incentives among patients could not be completely discarded. Then, the possibility of obtaining benefits associated to the malingerer role (e.g., economical compensation from health insurance companies, medical leave) was always latent. Both, increasing the size of future samples or using known-group comparison designs (Rogers, 2008) should be considered in further studies in order to improve the mentioned limitations of our studies.

Parallel to improving limitations of our previous studies, it would be of high scientific interest to include Brain-mapping techniques and contrast their findings with the results obtained using our Bayesian model. In this line, recent evidence has been found about the use of functional magnetic resonance imaging (fMRI) in malingering detection. For instance, Lee et al. (2009) implemented fMRI to distinguish errors from deceptive responses. More recently, Larsen, Allen, Bigler, Goodrich-Hunsaker, and Hopkins (2010) identified some specific patterns of brain activation in genuine and malingered effort.

From an interdisciplinary view, future research may combine the use of existing effort methods (e.g., SVT), Bayesian approaches and objective neuroimaging techniques to improve the way in which effort is evaluated in both clinical and medico-legal settings. This might open new research horizons that help us to better understand the malingering phenomenon from a behavioral, probabilistic or neurobiological perspectives. A holistic view of malingering and effort might bring better possibilities to develop more comprehensive assessment techniques.

# 6  LIST OF ABBREVIATIONS

| | |
|---|---|
| **2AFC** | two-alternatives forced-choice task |
| **AUC** | area under the curve |
| **CI** | cognitively impaired group |
| **EM** | experimental malingering group |
| **EVI** | embedded validity indicators |
| **HR** | honest responding group |
| **LR(+)** | likelihood ratio for a positive test result |
| **LR(-)** | likelihood ratio for a negative test result |
| **MCMC** | Markov chain Monte Carlo sampling method |
| **MND** | malingered neurocognitive disfunction |
| **NNF** | noncredible neurocognitive function |
| **NPV** | negative predictive value |
| **PPV** | positive predictive value |
| **SVT** | symptom validity testing |
| **SE** | symptom exaggeration group |
| **TBI** | traumatic brain injury |
| **TOMM** | Test of Memory Malingering |
| **WMT** | Word Memory Test |

# 7 REFERENCES

Ahn, W.-J., Krawitz, A., Kim, W., Busenmeyer, J. R., & Brown, J. W. (2011). A model-based fMRI analysis with hierarchical Bayesian parameter estimation. *Journal of Neuroscience, Psychology, and Economics, 4*, 95-110.

American Educational Research Association, American Psychological Association, National Council on Measurement in Education, Joint Committee on Standards for Educational, & Psychological Testing (US). (1999). *Standards for educational and psychological testing*. American Educational Research Association.

American Psychiatric Association. (1994). Diagnostic and Statistical Manual of Mental Disorders (4th ed.). Washington, DC: Author.

American Psychiatric Association. (2000). Diagnostic and Statistical Manual of Mental Disorders. 4th ed. Text revised. Washington, DC: Author.

Ardolf, B. R., Denney, R. L., & Houston, C. M. (2007). Base rates of negative response bias and malingered neurocognitive dysfunction among criminal defendants referred for neuropsychological evaluation. *The Clinical Neuropsychologist, 21*, 899-916.

Babikian, T., Boone, K. B., Lu, P., & Arnold, G. (2006). Sensitivity and specificity of various digit span scores in the detection of suspect effort. *The Clinical Neuropsychologist, 20*, 145-159.

Baker, G. A., Hanley, J. R., Jackson, H. F., Kimmance, S., & Slade, P. (1993). Detecting the faking of amnesia: performance differences between simulators and patients with memory impairment. *Journal of Clinical and Experimental Neuropsychology, 15*, 668-684.

Barrash, J., Suhr, J., & Manzel, K. (2004). Detecting poor effort and malingering with an expanded version of the auditory verbal learning test (AVLTX): Validation with clinical samples. *Journal of Clinical and Experimental Neuropsychology, 26*, 125-140.

Beetar, J. T., & Williams, J. M. (1995). Malingering Response Styles on the Memory Assessment Scales and Symptom Validity Tests. *Archives of Clinical Neuropsychology, 10,* 57-72.

Berry, D. T., Schipper, L. J. (2008). Assessment of Feigned Cognitive Impairment Using Standard Neuropsychological Tests. In Rogers, R. (2008). *Clinical assessment of malingering and deception* (3rd ed., pp. 237-252). New York: Guilford Press.

Bigler, E. D. (2012). Symptom validity testing, effort, and neuropsychological assessment. *Journal of the International Neuropsychological Society, 18,* 632-642.

Binder, L. M. (1993). Portland Digit Recognition Test manual (2nd ed.). Portland, OR: Private Publication.

Blaskewitz, N., Merten, T., & Brockhaus, R. (2009). Detection of suboptimal effort with the Rey Complex Figure Test and Recognition Trial. *Applied Neuropsychology, 16,* 54-61.

Bolan, B., Foster, J. K., Schmand, B., & Bolan, S. (2002). A comparison of three tests to detect feigned amnesia: the effects of feedback and the measurement of response latency. *Journal of Clinical and Experimental Neuropsychology, 24,* 154-167.

Boone, K. B., Lu, P., & Wen, J. (2005). Comparison of various RAVLT scores in the detection of noncredible memory performance. *Archives of Clinical Neuropsychology, 20,* 301-319.

Boone, K. B. (2007). A Reconsideration of the Slick et al. (1999) Criteria for Malingered Neurocognitive Dysfunction. In K. B. Boone (Ed.), *Assessment of feigned cognitive impairment: a neuropsychological perspective* (pp. 29-49). New York: Guilford Press.

Boone, K. B. (2011). *Assessment of response bias: Embedded effort indicators.* Presentation at the Second European Symposium on Symptom Validity Assessment, London.

Brennan, A., Meyer, S., David, E., Pella, R., Hill, B., & Gouvier, W. D. (2009). The Vulnerability to Coaching across Measures of Effort. *The Clinical Neuropsychologist, 23,* 314-328.

Brockhaus, R., & Merten, T. (2004). [Neuropsychological assessment of suboptimal performance: the Word Memory Test]. *Nervenarzt, 75,* 882-887.

Bush, S. S., Ruff, R. M., Troster, A. I., Barth, J. T., Koffler, S. P., Pliskin, N. H., et al. (2005). Symptom validity assessment: Practice issues and medical necessity - NAN policy & planning committee. *Archives of Clinical Neuropsychology, 20,* 419-426.

Campbell, R. J. (2009) Campbell's Psychiatric Dictionary: The Definitive Dictionary of Psychiatry (9th Ed.). Oxford University Press.

Cooter, R. (1998). Malingering in modernity: psychological scripts and adversial encounters during the First World War. In, R. Cooter, M. Harrison, and S. Sturdy (Eds.) *War medicine and modernity* (pp.125-148). Stroud: Sutton Publishing.

Dennis, S. J., Lee, M. D., & Kinnell, A. (2008). Bayesian analysis of recognition memory: The case of the list-length effect. *Journal of Memory and Language, 59,* 361-376.

Dienes, Z. (2011). Bayesian versus orthodox statistics: Which side are you on?. *Perspectives on Psychological Science, 6,* 274-290.

Dunn, T. M., Shear, P. K., Howe, S., & Ris, M. D. (2003). Detecting neuropsychological malingering: effects of coaching and information. *Archives of Clinical Neuropsychology, 18,* 121-134.

Etherton, J. L., Bianchini, K. J., Ciota, M. A., Heinly, M. T., & Greve, K. W. (2006). Pain, malingering and the WAIS-III Working Memory Index. *Spine Journal, 6,* 61-71.

Frederick, R.I. (1997). Validity Indicator Profile manual. Minnetonka, MN: NCS Assessments.

Frederick, R. I., & Speed, F. M. (2007). On the interpretation of below-chance responding in forced-choice tests. *Assessment, 14,* 3–11.

Gamerman, D., & Lopes, H. F. (2006). Markov chain Monte Carlo: Stochastic simulation for Bayesian inference, 2nd Ed. (Texts in Statistical Science Series). New York: Chapman & Hall/CRC.

Gerson, A., & Fox, D. (2006). Malingering. In J. E. Fisher & W. T. O'Donohue (Eds.), *Practitioner's guide to evidence based psychotherapy* (pp. 386-395). New York, NY: Springer.

Gilks, W. R., Richardson, S., & Spiegelhalter, D. J. (1996). Markov chain Monte Carlo in practice. Interdisciplinary Statistics, London: Chapman & Hall.

Glueck, B. (1916). The malingerer: a clinical study. *Criminal Science Monographs, 2,* 156-238.

Green, P. (2005). Word Memory Test for Windows: Test manual (revised June 2005). Edmonton, Alberta, Canada: Green's Publishing.

Grosz, H. J., & Zimmerman, J. (1965). Experimental analysis of hysterical blindness: A follow-up report and new experimental data. *Archives of General Psychiatry, 13,* 255-260.

Grote, C. L., Hook, J.N. (2007). Forced-Choice Recognition tests of Malingering. In G. J. Larrabee (Ed.), Assessment of malingered neuropsychological deficits (pp. 44-79). Oxford; New York: Oxford University Press.

Grove, W. M. (2005). Clinical versus statistical prediction: The contribution of Paul E. Meehl. *Journal of Clinical Psychology, 61,* 1233-1243.

Gunstad, J., & Suhr, J. A. (2001). Efficacy of the full and abbreviated forms of the Portland Digit Recognition Test: Vulnerability to coaching. *The Clinical Neuropsychologist, 15,* 397-404.

Hall, H. V., & Poirier, J. (2001). Detecting malingering and deception: Forensic distortion analysis: Boca Raton, Fla: CRC Press.

Halligan, P. W., Bass, C. M., & Oakley, D. A. (2003). Wilful deception as illness behaviour. In P. W. Halligan, C. M. Bass & D. A. Oakley (Eds.), *Malingering and Illness deception* (pp. 3-28). New York: Oxford University Press.

Hanley, J. R., Baker, G. A., & Ledson, S. (1999). Detecting the faking of amnesia: a comparison of the effectiveness of three different techniques for distinguishing simulators from patients with amnesia. Journal of Clinical and Experimental Neuropsychology, 21, 59-69.

Iverson, G. L. (2003). Detecting malngering in civil forensic evaluations. In A. M. N. Horton, Hartlage, L. C. (Eds.), Handbook of forensic neurpsychology (pp. 137-176). New York: Springer.

Iverson, G. L. (2006). Ethical issues associated with the assessment of exaggeration, poor effort, and malingering. Applied Neuropsychology, 13, 77-90.

Iverson, G. L. (2007). Identifying exaggeration and malingering. Pain Practice, 7, 94-102.

Iverson, G. L. (2008). Assessing for exaggeration, poor effort and malingering in neuropsychological assessment. In Horton, A. M. N., Wedding, D. (Eds.), The neuropsychology handbook (3rd ed., pp. 125-182): Springer Pub.

Iverson, G. L. (2010). Assessing for exaggeration, poor effort and malingering in neuropsychological assessment. In A. M. N. Horton, Hartlage, L. C. (Eds.), Handbook of forensic neurpsychology (2nd ed., pp. 91-135). New York: Springer.

Iverson, G., & Binder, L. (2000). Detecting exaggeration and malingering in neuropsychological assessment. Journal of Head Trauma Rehabilitation, 15, 829-858.

Jaynes, E. T. (2003). Probability theory: The logic of science. Cambridge: Cambridge University Press.

Jeffreys, H. (1961). Theory of probability (3rd ed.). Oxford: Clarendon Press.

Jones, R., Anderson, S., Cole, T., & Hathaway-Nepple, J. (1996). Neuropsychological sequelae of traumatic brain injury. In M. Rizzo & D. Tranel (Eds.), Head injury and postconcussive syndrome (pp. 395-414). New York: Churchill Livingstone.

Kim, M. S., Boone, K. B., Victor, T., Marion, S. D., Amano, S., Cottingham, M. E., et al. (2010). The Warrington Recognition Memory Test for Words as a Measure of Response Bias: Total Score and Response Time Cutoffs Developed on "Real

World" Credible and Noncredible Subjects. *Archives of Clinical Neuropsychology, 25,* 60-70.

Kruschke, J. K., & John, K. (2010). Doing Bayesian data analysis: A tutorial introduction with R and BUGS. Burlington, MA: Academic Press/Elsevier.

Lange, R. T., Sullivan, K., & Anderson, D. (2005). Ecological validity of the WMS-III rarely missed index in personal injury litigation. *Journal of Clinical and Experimental Neuropsychology, 27,* 412-424.

Lange, R. T., Iverson, G. L., Sullivan, K., & Anderson, D. (2006). Suppressed working memory on the WMS-III as a marker for poor effort. *Journal of Clinical and Experimental Neuropsychology, 28,* 294-305.

Lange, R. T., Pancholi, S., Bhagwat, A., Anderson-Barnes, V., & French, L. M. (2012). Influence of poor effort on neuropsychological test performance in US military personnel following mild traumatic brain injury. *Journal of Clinical and Experimental Neuropsychology, 34,* 453-466.

Larrabee, G. (2003). Detection of malingering using atypical performance patterns on standard neuropsychological tests. *The Clinical Neuropsychologist, 17,* 410-425.

Larrabee, G. (2007). Malingering, research designs, and base rates. In G. Larrabee (Ed.), *Assessment of malingered neuropsychological deficits* (pp. xiv, 386 p.). Oxford; New York: Oxford University Press.

Larrabee, G. J., Greiffenstein, M. F., Grewe, K. W., & Bianchini, K. J. (2007). Refining Diagnostic Criteria for Malingering. In G. J. Larrabee (Ed.), *Assessment of malingered neuropsychological deficits* (pp. 334-371). Oxford; New York: Oxford University Press.

Larrabee, G. J., Millis, S. R., & Meyers, J. E. (2008). Sensitivity to brain dysfunction of the Halstead-Reitan vs an ability-focused neuropsychological battery. *The Clinical Neuropsychologist, 22,* 813-825.

Larsen, J. D., Allen, M. D., Bigler, E. D., Goodrich-Hunsaker, N. J., & Hopkins, R. O. (2010). Different patterns of cerebral activation in genuine and malingered cognitive effort during performance on the Word Memory Test. *Brain Injury, 24,* 89-99.

Lee, M. D. (2010). How cognitive modeling can benefit from hierarchical Bayesian models. *Journal of Mathematical Psychology, 55,* 1-7.

Lee, M. D., & Wagenmakers, E.-J. (2010). A course in Bayesian graphical modeling for cognitive science: Unpublished course materials. Retrieved October 05, 2010, from http://www.ejwagenmakers.com/BayesCourse/BayesBookWeb.pdf.

Lee, M. D., Wagenmakers, E.-J. (2013). Inferences with Binomials. In M. D. Lee, & E.-J., Wagenmakers (Eds.), *Bayesian Cognitive Modeling: A Practical Course* (pp. 37-53). Cambridge University Press.

Lee, T. M. C., Au, R. K. C., Liu, H. L., Ting, K. H., Huang, C. M., & Chan, C. C. H. (2009). Are errors differentiable from deceptive responses when feigning memory impairment? An fMRI study. *Brain and Cognition, 69,* 406-412.

Loring, D. W., Larrabee, G. J., Lee, G. P., & Meador, K. J. (2007). Victoria symptom validity test performance in a heterogenous clinical sample. *The Clinical Neuropsychologist, 21,* 522-531.

Lu, P. H., Boone, K. B., Cozolino, L., & Mitchell, C. (2003). Effectiveness of the Rey-Osterrieth complex figure test and the Meyers and Meyers Recognition Trial in the detection of suspect effort. *The Clinical Neuropsychologist, 17,* 426-440.

Lunn, D. J., Thomas, A., Best, N., & Spiegelhalter, D. (2000). WinBUGS a Bayesian modelling framework: Concepts, structure, and extensibility. *Statistics and Computing, 10,* 325-337.

Lunn, D., Spiegelhalter, D., Thomas, A., & Best, N. (2009). The BUGS project: Evolution, critique and future directions. *Statistics in Medicine, 28,* 3049-3067.

Macmillan, N., & Creelman, C. (2008). Detection theory: A user's guide (2nd ed.). New Jersey: Lawrence Erlbaum.

Mendelson, G., & Mendelson, D. (2004). Malingering pain in the medicolegal context. *The Clinical Journal of Pain, 20,* 423-432.

Merckelbach, H., Smeets, T., & Jelicic, M. (2009). Experimental simulation: type of malingering scenario makes a difference. *Journal of Forensic Psychiatry & Psychology, 20,* 378-386.

Merten, T., Friedel, E., Mehren, G., & Stevens, A. (2007). Über die validität von persönlichkeitsprofilen in der nervenärztlichen begutachtung [Negative response bias and the validity of personality profiles in neuropsychiatric assessment]. *Nervenartz, 78,* 511-520.

Miller, L. (1996). Malingering in mild head injury and postconcussion syndrome: clinical, neuropsychological and forensic consideration. *Journal of Cognitive Rehabilitation, 14,* 6–17.

Miller, L., Boyd, M., Cohn, A., Wilson, J., & McFarland, M. (2006). Prevalence of sub-optimal effort in disability applicants. Paper presented at the 34th annual meeting of the International Neuropsychological Society, Boston.

Millis, S. R. (1994). Assessment of motivation and memory with the Recognition Memory Test after financially compensable mild head injury. *Journal of Clinical Psychology, 50,* 601-605.

Millis, S. (2008). What clinicians really need to know about symptom exaggeration, insufficient effort, and malingering: Statistical and measurement matters. In J. E. Morgan, & J. J. Sweet (Eds.), *Neuropsychology of malingering casebook* (pp. 21-37). Hove, East Sussex: Psychology Press.

Mittenberg, W., Patton, C., Canyock, E., & Condit, D. (2002). Base Rates of Malingering and Symptom Exeggeration. *Journal of Clinical and Experimental Neuropsychology, 24,* 1094-1102.

Morel, K. R., & Shepherd, B. E. (2008). Developing a symptom validity test for posttraumatic stress disorder: Application of the binomial distribution. *Journal of Anxiety Disorders, 22,* 1297-1302.

Mossman, D. (2000). The meaning of malingering data: Further applications of Bayes' theorem. *Behavioral Sciences & the Law, 18,* 761-779.

Mossman, D., & Hart, K. J. (1996). Presenting evidence of malingering to courts: Insights from decision theory. *Behavioral Sciences & the Law, 14,* 271-291.

Mossman, D., Wygant, D. B., & Gervais, R. O. (2012). Estimating the accuracy of neurocognitive effort measures in the absence of a "gold standard". *Psychological assessment, 24,* 815-822.

Nagle, A. M., Everhart, D. E., Durham, T. W., McCammon, S. L., & Walker, M. (2006). Deception strategies in children: Examination of forced choice recognition and verbal learning and memory techniques. *Archives of Clinical Neuropsychology, 21,* 777-785.

Nicholson, K., & Martelli, M. F. (2007). Malingering: Overview and basic concepts. In G. Young, Kane, A. W., Nicholson, K., & Shuman, D. W. (Ed.), *Causality of psychological injury: presenting evidence in court* (pp. 375-401). New York: Springer.

Nilsson, H., Rieskamp, J., & Wagenmakers, E.-J. (2010). Hierarchical Bayesian parameter estimation for cumulative prospect theory. *Journal of Mathematical Psychology, 55,* 84-93.

O'Hagan, A., Forster, J., & Kendall, M. G. (1994). Bayesian inference: Edward Arnold London.

O'Hagan, A., & Forster, J. J. (2004). Kendall's Advanced Theory of Statistics, Volume 2B: Bayesian inference (2nd ed.). London: Arnold.

Ortega, A., Wagenmakers, E.-J., Lee, M. D., Markowitsch, H. J., & Piefke, M. (2012). A Bayesian latent group analysis for detecting poor effort in the assessment of malingering. *Archives of Clinical Neuropsychology, 27,* 453-465.

Ortega, A., Labrenz, S., Markowitsch, H. J., & Piefke, M. (2013). Diagnostic Accuracy of a Bayesian Latent Group Analysis for the Detection of Malingering-Related Poor Effort. The Clinical Neuropsychologist, 27, 1019-1042.

Ortega, A., Piefke, M., & Markowitsch, H. J. (2014). A Bayesian latent group analysis for detecting poor effort in a sample of cognitively impaired patients. Journal of clinical and experimental neuropsychology, 36, 659-667.

Palmer, I. P. (2003). Malingering, shirking, and self-inflicted injuries in the military. In P. W. Halligan, C. M. Bass & D. A. Oakley (Eds.), *Malingering and illness deception* (pp. 42-53). New York: Oxford University Press.

Palmer, I. P. (2006). Military and Mass Hysteria. In Hallett, M., Cloninger, C. R., Fahn, S., Jankovic, J., Lang, A. E., & Yudofsky, S. C. (2005). *Psychogenic movement disorders: neurology and neuropsychiatry* (pp. 20-23). Lippincott Williams & Wilkins.

Pankratz, L., Fausti, S. A., & Peed, S. (1975). Forced-Choice Technique to Evaluate Deafness in Hysterical or Malingering Patient. *Journal of Consulting and Clinical Psychology, 43,* 421-422.

Piefke, M., Onur, Ö. A., & Fink, G. R. (2012). Aging-related changes of neural mechanisms underlying visual-spatial working memory. *Neurobiology of Aging, 33,* 1284-1297.

Piefke, M., Weiss, P.H., Zilles, K., Markowitsch, H.J., & Fink, G.R. (2003). Differential remoteness and emotional tone modulate the neural correlates of autobiographical memory. *Brain, 126,* 650-668.

Resnick, P. J. (1984). The detection of malingered mental illness. *Behavioral Sciences & the Law, 2,* 21-38.

Resnick, P. J. (1997). Malingering of posttraumatic disorders. In R. Rogers (Ed.), *Clinical assessment of malingering and deception* (2nd ed., pp. 130-152). New York: Guilford Press.

Rogers, R. (1988). Current status of clinical methods. In R. Rogers (Ed) *Clinical assessment of malingering and deception* (pp. 293-308). New York: Guilford.

Rogers, R. (1990). Development of a new classification model of malingering. *Bulletin American Academy of Psychiatry and the Law, 18,* 323-333.

Rogers, R. (2008). Clinical assessment of malingering and deception (3rd ed.). New York: Guilford Press.

Rogers, R., Sewell, K. W., & Goldstein, A. M. (1994). Explanatory Models of Malingering: a Prototypical Analysis. *Law and Human Behavior,* 18, 543-552.

Rogers, R., Salekin, R., Sewell, K., Goldstein, A., & Leonard, K. (1998). A comparison of forensic and nonforensic malingerers: A prototypical analysis of explanatory models. *Law and Human Behavior, 22,* 353-367.

Rogers, R., & Salekin, R. T. (1998). Research report beguiled by Bayes: A re-analysis of Mossman and Hart's estimates of malingering. *Behavioral Sciences & the Law, 16,* 147-153.

Rohling, M. L., Allen, L. M., & Green, P. (2002). Who is exaggerating cognitive impairment and who is not? *CNS Spectrums, 7,* 387-395.

Rosenfeld, B., Sands, S. A., & Van Gorp, W. G. (2000). Have we forgotten the base rate problem? Methodological issues in the detection of distortion. *Archives of Clinical Neuropsychology, 15,* 349-359.

Samaniego, F. J. (2010). A comparison of the Bayesian and Frequentist approaches to estimation. New York: Springer.

Schagen, S., Schmand, B., de Sterke, S., & Lindeboom, J. (1997). Amsterdam Short-Term Memory Test: A new procedure for the detection of feigned memory deficits. *Journal of Clinical and Experimental Neuropsychology, 19,* 43-51.

Schulte-Rüther, M., Markowitsch, H. J., Fink, G. R., & Piefke, M. (2007). Mirror neuron and theory of mind mechanisms involved in face-to-face interactions: A functional magnetic resonance imaging approach to empathy. *Journal of Cognitive Neuroscience, 19,* 1354-1372.

Shiffrin, R. M., Lee, M. D., Kim, W., & Wagenmakers, E.-J. (2008). A survey of model evaluation approaches with a tutorial on hierarchical Bayesian methods. *Cognitive Science, 32,* 1248-1284.

Siegel, S. (1956). Nonparametric methods for the behavioral sciences. New York.

Slick, D., Hopp, G., Strauss, E., & Thompson, G. (1997). VSVT: Victoria Symptom Validity Test. *Odessa, Florida: Psychological Assessment Resources.*

Slick, D., Sherman, E., & Iverson, G. (1999). Diagnostic criteria for malingered neurocognitive dysfunction: Proposed standards for clinical practice and research. *The Clinical Neuropsychologist, 13,* 545-561.

Slick, D. J., Tan, J. E., Strauss, E., Mateer, C. A., Harnadek, M., & Sherman, E. M. (2003). Victoria Symptom Validity Test scores of patients with profound memory impairment: nonlitigants case studies. *The Clinical Neuropsychologist, 17,* 390-394.

Spreen, O., & Benton, A. L. (1963). Simulation of mental deficiency on a visual memory test. *American Journal of Mental Deficiency, 67,* 909-913.

Steyvers, M., Tenenbaum, J. B., Wagenmakers, E.-J., & Blum, B. (2003). Inferring causal networks from observations and interventions. *Cognitive Science, 27*, 453-489.

Streiner, D. (2003). Diagnosing tests: Using and misusing diagnostic and screening tests. *Journal of Personality Assessment, 81*, 209-219.

Sullivan, K., Lange, R. T., & Dawes, S. (2005). Methods of detecting malingering and estimated symptom exaggeration base rates in Australia. *Journal of forensic neuropsychology, 4*, 49-70.

Sullivan, B. K., May, K., & Galbally, L. (2007). Symptom exaggeration by college adults in attention-deficit hyperactivity disorder and learning disorder assessments. *Applied Neuropsychology, 14*, 189-207.

Sweet, J., Condit, D., & Nelson, N. (2008). Feigned Amnesia and Memory Loss. In Rogers, R. (2008). *Clinical assessment of malingering and deception* (3rd ed., pp.218-236 ). New York: Guilford Press.

Tenenbaum, J. B., Griffiths, T. L., & Kemp, C. (2006). Theory-based Bayesian models of inductive learning and reasoning. Trends in Cognitive Science, 10, 309-318.

Tombaugh, T. N. (1996). Test of Memory Malingering TOMM. New York: Multi-Health Systems.

Verschuere, B., Meijer, E., & Crombez, G. (2008). Symptom Validity Testing for the detection of simulated amnesia: Not robust to coaching. *Psychology, Crime & Law, 14*, 523-528.

Vickery, C.D., Berry, D.T., Inman, T.H., Harris, M.J., & Orey, S.A. (2001). Detection of inadequate effort on neuropsychological testing: A meta-analytic review of selected procedures. *Archives of Clinical Neuropsychology, 16*, 45-73.

Vrij, A. (2001). Detecting the liars. *The Psychologist. 14*, 596-598.

Walters, G. D., Berry, D. T. R., Lanyon, R. I., & Murphy, M. P. (2009). Are exaggerated health complaints continuous or categorical? A taxometric analysis of the health problem overstatement scale. *Psychological Assessment, 21*, 219-226.

Walters, G. D., Rogers, R., Berry, D. T. R., Miller, H. A., Duncan, S. A., McCusker, P. J., et al. (2008). Malingering as a categorical or dimensional construct: The latent structure of feigned psychopathology as measured by the SIRS and MMPI-2. *Psychological Assessment, 20,* 238-247

Wessely, S. (2003). Malingering: historical perspectives. In P. W. Halligan, C. M. Bass & D. A. Oakley (Eds.), *Malingering and illness deception* (pp. 31-41). New York: Oxford University Press.

Wiggins, E. C., & Brandt, J. (1988). The Detection of Simulated Amnesia. *Law and Human Behavior, 12,* 57-78.

Young, G. A., & Smith, R. L. (2005). Decision Theory. In G. A. Young & R. L. Smith (Eds.), *Essentials of statistical inference* (pp. 4-21). New York: Cambridge University Press.

Zago, S., Sartori, G., & Scarlato, G. (2004). Malingering and retrograde amnesia: the historic case of the Collegno amnesic. *Cortex, 40,* 519-532

Zielinski, J. J. (1994). Malingering and defensiveness in the neuropsychological assessment of mild traumatic brain injury. *Clinical Psychology: Science and Practice, 1,* 169-183.

# 8 TECHNICAL APPENDIX

## Technical Appendix

To replicate our findings, the interested reader needs to work with the software WinBUGS (http://www.mrc-bsu.cam.ac.uk/bugs/) through the software R (http://cran.opensourceresources.org/). A good tutorial about how to install WinBUGS and R can be found in:

http://www.ejwagenmakers.com/BayesCourse/BayesBookWeb.pdf.

In Chapter 2, a detailed description of the required steps to make these applications work together can be found.

## How to import the raw data into R and WinBUGS?

Two different files are used, a) the model and b) the data file. The first one contains the specifications and assumptions of the model, in this case the Bayesian Latent Group Analysis of Malingering. Copy the model file **(Appendix A)** and save it as plain text file (.txt)*. The data file contains the raw scores, number of trials and the path to the defined R working directory. Copy the data file **(Appendix B)**, open the R console and paste it directly on it. Then, replace the information contained in the Appendix B **(bold text)** with your own data and save the new file in R extension (i.e., my_data_file.R). Save both, the model and the data files in the same folder . Finally, run your R file and wait for WinBUGS to return the output.

After providing all the required inputs (raw scores, number of trials, path to the folders, etc.) the information is sent to WinBUGS where the Bayesian analysis is performed. WinBUGS returns the output that is automatically shown in your screen. The output file can be saved in different file formats.

*For any question regarding R or WinBUGS see the above-mentioned tutorial.

# Appendix A: Model File

```
# BALGAM: BAyesian Latent Group Assessment of Malingering. Assumption: two groups, #bona fide
participants (bon) and malingerers (mal). Every participant has a success #rate that is
determined by group membership; So all malingerers have a relatively low #success rate, and
all bona fide # participants have a relatively high success rate.


model

{

  # Each Person Belongs To One Of Two Latent Groups, Either BON or MAL

  for (i in 1:p)

  {

     z[i]    ~ dbern(phi) # phi is the Base Rate

     z1[i] <- z[i]+1

  }

  # Relatively Uninformative Prior on Base Rate for Naive Malingerers

  phi ~ dbeta(5,5)

  # Data Follow Binomial With Rate Given By Each Person's Group Assignment

  for (i in 1:p)

  {

    k[i]       ~ dbin(theta[i,z1[i]],n)

    theta[i,1] ~ dbeta(alpha[1],beta[1])

    theta[i,2] ~ dbeta(alpha[2],beta[2])

  }

  # Transformation to Group Mean and Precision

  alpha[1] <- mu_bon * lambda_bon

  beta[1]  <- lambda_bon * (1-mu_bon)

  # Additivity on Logit Scale

  logit(mu_mal) <- logit(mu_bon) - mu_diff


  alpha[2] <- mu_mal * lambda_mal

  beta[2]  <- lambda_mal * (1-mu_mal)

  # Priors

  mu_bon   ~ dbeta(1,1)

  mu_diff ~ dnorm(0,0.5)I(0,) # Constrained to be Postive


  lambda_bon ~ dunif(40,800)

  lambda_mal ~ dunif(4,100)

}
```

## Appendix B: Data File

```
# clears workspace:
rm(list=ls(all=TRUE))


#Here replace the existing path and type in the path to your working directory:
setwd("C:\Dokumente und Einstellungen\Administrator\Eigene Dateien")


# The library (R2WinBuGS) must be loaded on "R" when running the analysis.
library(R2WinBUGS)


#Here type in the location in which WinBUGS is installed on your computer
bugsdir = "C:/Programme/WinBUGS14"


#Data of bona fide group vs. coached malingerers. Here you can insert your data set.
k = c(45,45,44,45,44,45,45,45,45,45,30,20,6,44,44,27,25,17,14,27,35,30)
p = length(k) # number of people
#Here you can change the number of trials
n = 45          # number of trials


data  = list("p", "k", "n") # to be passed on to WinBUGS
myinits = list(
  list(z = round(runif(p)), mu.diff=0.2),
  list(z = round(runif(p)), mu.diff=0.3),
  list(z = round(runif(p)), mu.diff=0.4))


# parameters to be monitored:
parameters = c("theta","z","mu.bon","lambda.bon",
               "mu.mal","lambda.mal","mu.diff","phi")


# The following command calls WinBUGS with specific options.
# For a detailed description see Sturtz, Ligges, & Gelman (2005).
samples = bugs(data, inits=myinits, parameters,
               model.file ="my_model_file_here.txt",
               n.chains=3, n.iter=10000, n.burnin=1000, n.thin=1,
               DIC=T, bugs.directory=bugsdir,
               codaPkg=F, debug=T)
```

.